Praise for
Born Royal

"In her book *Born Royal*, Oneka McClellan encourages each of us to join a royal sisterhood by letting go of our insecurities and fully embracing our position as the loved-beyond-measure daughters of the King. I have seen her walk out this journey, and I know her words will encourage you!"

—HOLLY WAGNER, author of
Find Your Brave and founder of She Rises

"Oneka McClellan reminds women that we have been created uniquely and intentionally, on purpose and for a purpose. When we know our true worth and belonging, we live and love from confidence, not comparison. The moment is now to rise up and live crowned for such a time as this!"

—MADISON PREWETT TROUTT, bestselling author of
The Love Everybody Wants

"Be inspired to walk confidently and securely in who you have been created to be, while cultivating the same growth in other women as well. We don't have to allow the dysfunctional ways society have normalized for women to determine how we behave as chosen Christ followers. We are challenged to be the biggest cheerleaders of other women and pass down biblical and practical knowledge to generations that follow. Be prepared to be forever changed for the better and evolve into the reality of what it means to be Born Royal!"

—IRENE ROLLINS, co-founder of Two Equals One marriage
ministry and author of *Reframe Your Shame*

"*Born Royal* is a call for the women of our generation to step into our true identity as daughters of the King. Chosen, prepared, and crowned to say a confident *yes* to all that God intends for them."

—JENNIE LUSKO, pastor of Fresh Life Church with her husband, Levi, and bestselling author of *The Fight to Flourish*

"*Born Royal* is a God-breathed vision for women of every generation to no longer settle for any lesser label than 'daughters of the King.' McClellan's journey is an impartation of hard-earned wisdom from God's Word and an infusion of encouragement—from the queen of encouragement herself."

—JULIE MULLINS, senior pastor of Christ Fellowship Church

"Oneka McClellan is the world's greatest cheerleader. You will be inspired, equipped, and compelled to step into all God has created you to be and do all He has placed you on the earth to do."

—CHRISTINE CAINE, founder of the A21 Campaign and Propel Women

"In *Born Royal,* Oneka McClellan does what she does best—she reminds us of who we are and whose we are, and she compels us toward all we can be. If you're ready to step into all God says you are—read this book!"

—SHELLEY GIGLIO, co-founder of the Passion Movement and Passion City Church

Born Royal

Born Royal

OVERCOMING INSECURITY TO BECOME
THE WOMAN GOD SAYS YOU ARE

ONEKA MCCLELLAN

Foreword by Lisa Harper

WaterBrook

LIBRARY OF CONGRESS CATALOGING-IN-PUBLICATION DATA

Names: McClellan, Oneka, author.
Title: Born royal: overcoming insecurity to become the woman
God says you are / Oneka McClellan.
Description: Colorado Springs: WaterBrook, [2024] |
Includes bibliographical references.
Identifiers: LCCN 2023035963 | ISBN 9780593445686
(hardcover; acid-free paper) | ISBN 9780593600627 (eISBN)
Subjects: LCSH: Christian women, | Christian life. | Women and religion.
Classification: LCC BV4527 .M368 2024 |
DDC 248.8/43—dc23/eng/20240112
LC record available at https://lccn.loc.gov/2023035963

Printed in the United States of America on acid-free paper

waterbrookmultnomah.com

2 4 6 8 9 7 5 3 1

First Edition

Most WaterBrook books are available at special quantity discounts for bulk purchase for premiums, fundraising, and corporate and educational needs by organizations, churches, and businesses. Special books or book excerpts also can be created to fit specific needs. For details, contact specialmarketscms@penguinrandomhouse.com.

I'll never forget the day I met Oneka McClellan. We were filming a Propel Women curriculum with Christine Caine in California, and Oneka came walking into the studio with kind eyes and a big, warm smile. I found myself thinking, *Wow, for such a beautiful woman, she sure does seem nice.* Not that physical beauty and kindness are always mutually exclusive in women, but I've met a few whose grace doesn't match their selfie face yet!

Within a few minutes, we started filming. For whatever reason, the production team had us perched on high stools under bright lights. I already tend to sweat profusely on camera, but because on this day I was also preoccupied with trying to stay put and not slide off the stool, I was a tad distracted when Chris asked us to share something God had recently been teaching us. Oneka answered, saying something that snapped both my head and my heart in her direction. She said, "I want to be a 'there you are' kind of person, not the 'here I am' kind." I'd never heard humility synopsized so simply and profoundly before.

In the decade since that first encounter, Oneka has become a very dear friend whom I love to laugh with and learn from. Her clear and passionate delivery of the gospel onstage is more than matched by her transparency and compassion offstage. Her *orthodoxy* (what she believes to be true about God and His Word) is genuinely reflected in her *orthopraxy* (how she lives because of what she believes to be true about God and His Word). This Spirit-led union of authority and authenticity is a stunning reminder that being a daughter of the King of all kings compels us to be both royal *and* humble—upright in our ethics yet willing to get low enough to wash one another's feet.

However, all it takes is a brief scroll through social media and it becomes apparent that humility is not exactly trending! I think there's so much emphasis in postmodernity, on branding and influencing, that we've all but forgotten that being God's beloved daughters often comes at the cost of popularity, that loosening the white-knuckled grip on our rights and our reputation is an inherent part of being shaped like Jesus.

Of course, it's easy to post humble-brags on Instagram, but it's a whole other thing to live a life bent toward God and other-oriented service, to be "there you are" carriers of the gospel instead of "here I am" consumers. And to emulate our Savior's posture when He gave His disciples a Passover pedicure, knowing full well Judas had already sold Him out and the three closest to Him—Peter, James, and John—would soon fall asleep while He travailed in the Garden of Gethsemane, just prior to the Crucifixion.

As we soak in the wisdom our Creator Redeemer has poured through Oneka onto every page of this beautiful book, let's not forget that our Savior—the One we're called to emulate—willingly laid down His scepter in glory and acquiesced to death on a cross to wash our prone-to-wander hearts clean from sin with His blood. Let's endeavor to lean into the royalty we've inherited by His grace—not earned by our behavior—with real humility and radical gratitude!

—Lisa Harper, speaker, Bible teacher, and author of *Life* and *Jesus*

Contents

INTRODUCTION

Almost every woman we meet, from the playground to the board-room, hides a deeper story of broken friendship, insecurity, betrayal, unmet expectations, and feelings of abandonment. Sadly, we live in a world where these struggles are almost unavoid-able. And the flip side is true too: At some point in our imperfect lives, nearly every one of us has torn another woman down or allowed a friend to gossip to us about someone when we should have been speaking words of life and encouragement over the women around us.

Born Royal isn't just a catchphrase; rather, this is a movement, a value revolution of everyday women who are passionate about being a part of bringing heaven to earth. Passionate about turning the tide of comparison and competition and criticism. And passionate about lifting one another up instead of tearing one another down. Even as we navigate our own insecurities, a part of us is longing to bring hope and healing to our world today and to the next generation.

I think it's time to break the mold of what we've been pressured to be. It's time to break the box we've been locked in.

> *It's time to put behind us*
> *what* should be *and step*
> *into what* could be.

What if we celebrated women of all backgrounds and walked with our heads held high instead of taking ourselves for granted? What if we began to see ourselves the way Christ sees us? What if we lived as though our royalty was not just a thing in storybooks or a position for a select few but a posture of the heart and a way of life?

Because here's the truth: It's about *who* you are, not just *what* you are.

If I start living into the fullness of who God has called me to be and if you start living into the fullness of who God has called you to be, then together we start a movement. A movement that grows and grows to become a sisterhood.

As a sisterhood, we can commit to standing up for the women in our lives and also for ourselves. As royal women, we can lean in to strengthen and lift up girls of all ages in our communities, in our churches, and all around the globe.

And I am telling you now that you are a part of this movement.

It begins with each of us agreeing to a set of shared values and principles and declaring that we will embrace our worth, stand up for other women, and refuse to stop being forces of good in the world. We won't stop fighting this uphill battle until every woman is loved and valued for who she truly is, for the beauty inside her. But we're not doing this alone. God goes before us and has shown us the simple yet powerful way this is done.

Micah 5:1 says, "Gather yourself in troops, O daughter of troops; a state of siege has been placed against us" (AMP). This is unfortunately and horrifically true today. We are under siege in every area of our culture, from brutal bullying in schools to the horrendous crimes committed against women. Like it or not, we're engaged in a war, my friend. But the divisive plan of the Enemy to sow enmity in our ranks has been exposed by the work of Jesus, and we can rise up against it, as daughters of God. We have the opportunity to join forces and sing a new anthem, which will send ripples of love and acceptance out into the world, and our song won't be silenced.

We will know we're living into our royalty when we realize our limitless value and recognize the same in every woman we meet as we walk this planet. We will live in our royal identity when, as a company of God's daughters, we encourage and fan the flames of life and purpose in one another. Can you imagine? How powerful could this company become if girls in middle school and high school watched out for one another and defended classmates who were being bullied? The royal sisterhood will be on display when college girls love and accept one another, when both stay-at-home moms and working moms notice the inherent strength in one another and call it out for the whole world to see. The royal sister-hood will be at work when we develop a deep passion for praying for one another like we never have before.

Think about it like this: You and I have been selected by God to be alive at this very moment in history. You and I were born for such a time as this—we're here for a very real, eternal reason. Instead of competing with one another or arguing about politics or parenting or how to school our children, let's commit to encouraging and speaking life over the women around us.

The time for this kind of out-loud faith is right now. This movement starts with each of us. This movement starts with *you*.

So join me. Let's set our faces like flint and turn our hearts toward heaven. We will be a part of bringing heaven to earth in our own communities! We will rise up when it's easy, and we will rise up when it's difficult and uncomfortable. We will stand on the shoulders of the men and women who came before us in this fight, and in doing so, we will honor their contributions and sacrifice. We will speak for those who can't speak for themselves, commit to lifting up the name of Jesus, and invite every woman we meet to join us on the journey.

It's my prayer that this book would inspire you to join this movement, heart and soul. These pages are filled with words that I'm praying and believing will till the soil of your heart. Then a seed of change can take root, sprout, and grow, causing you and the women in your world to flourish. I believe in you, I love you, and "I will not stop praying for [you] until [your] righteousness shines likes the dawn" (Isaiah 62:1)!

Born Royal

1

YOUR TIME IS NOW

I remember when I became a mom. I remember what I thought it would look like. I remember all the things I saw in magazines (there was no Instagram at the time), and I remember seeing moms fit back in their jeans two days to two weeks after giving birth. I remember everyone telling me how incredible it would be and all the love I would have and how I would fall more in love with my husband. And all those things are true.

But what I didn't know, what no one told me, was how sleep deprivation would turn into anxiety. No one told me that our firstborn would cry for no reason or that I would hear crying even when he wasn't. No one told me how hard my first day of solo parenting would be when my husband went back to work. No one told me how difficult breastfeeding could be or about the challenges of recovering from a C-section while also caring for one of the greatest gifts in my life. My reality was the opposite of the pictures I saw, the opposite of the stories I was told. I felt like a failure because my life wasn't matching up to the examples I saw in magazines.

So do you make it through the sleepless nights? You sure do. Do you eventually get your body back? It's totally possible in many cases. But is it still hard eighteen years in? Heck, yes. Is it the most rewarding delight and the joy of my heart? You'd better believe it. I say all of this not to scare you but to prepare you for when what you face is the opposite of what you feel prepared for. You'll be stronger on the other side. You'll be able to hold the hand of moms that come after you, and you'll wake up a new kind of fight and determination that you never knew you had.

For many of us, the tension we carry every day is deep and painful. Maybe we don't know what we'll encounter at home, at work, or at school from a roommate, friend, spouse, boyfriend, or colleague. We might feel confident and strong one day, while on other days we'll feel overwhelmed and think, *I'm going to sink under all this pressure!* Can you relate?

For some of us, this pressure manifests in our own minds, in our thoughts. Many of us battle negative thinking constantly, especially in today's world, in which we're bombarded by bad news—it comes at us from all sides. On the outside, we might look like we're doing just fine, but inside, our minds are waging war. In fact, we may feel the physical effects of all this negativity in our bodies, with our health taking a hit. One day we might receive a positive health report from the doctor, and we feel fantastic. But after a particularly stressful season, we might receive a very different report on our health. We all face struggles in different ways.

The Bible gives us story after story of how God showed up for people who felt unprepared.

When Joshua took over the leadership of Israel after Moses

died, God told him, "Be strong and courageous! Do not be afraid or discouraged. For the LORD your God is with you wherever you go" (Joshua 1:9).

To the Israelites taken captive and forced to live in the Babylonian Empire far from their homeland, who surely felt unprepared for and confused about their new life, God said, "I know the plans I have for you. . . . They are plans for good and not for disaster, to give you a future and a hope. In those days when you pray, I will listen" (Jeremiah 29:11–12).

When the angel Gabriel appeared to Mary, she felt confused and disturbed about how her life may be changing, but the angel had said, "Don't be afraid, Mary" (Luke 1:30) and promised the Holy Spirit would come to her (verse 35).

And when Jesus ascended, leaving the disciples to carry out His work on earth with the Holy Spirit—and can you imagine the state of their emotions?—Jesus reassured them: "Be sure of this: I am with you always, even to the end of the age" (Matthew 28:20).

I give the same message to you, reader: God is with *you*.

God is with you.

He's with you on your good days and your bad days. He's with you when you have it all together and when you feel like you're about to lose your mind. Sometimes you just have to know that God is with you and that He is there to bring you peace, grace, strength, and hope. God also reminds you that no matter what battle you are currently facing or will face in the future, He sent His Son in the form of a baby, and this promise is just as relevant to your life today as it was yesterday. I think sometimes we forget about the hope of the world: Jesus is here with us now.

The road wasn't easy for Joshua, the Israelites, Mary, or the disciples, but what might have felt like the wrong time was truly the right time.

I love Galatians 4:4: "When the right time came, God sent his Son, born of a woman." Look at that first part: "When the right time came."

When I read those words, I recalled the time many years ago when God placed a dream in both my husband, Earl, and me to plant a church. While we were on staff at a church in Austin, a business leader came up to us and said, "I feel like you guys are supposed to go to this conference." It was prophetic. He continued, "I just feel like I'm supposed to pay your way to go to London." This offer was an out-of-the-blue blessing. My mother-in-law then paid for us to take our son, Parker, who was five years old at the time. So Earl and I packed our bags, bundled up our son, and caught a flight to London.

The first night we were there, Earl woke up in the middle of the night, having had a dream. He turned to me and said, "This sounds crazy, honestly, but I feel like we're supposed to start a church."

"I've known that since I met you in college," I responded. "I'm so glad you got that revelation."

But we waited a few years before we moved on that dream to plant our church, Shoreline City Church. We could have gone to Dallas prematurely, but we waited and prayed and planned, then went at the appointed time. At just the right time, God assembled a team. At just the right time, He provided finances, volunteers, and more. At just the right time, He provided a movie theater when we needed a second building. At just the right time, He provided a cute little church on Town North when we needed a third building. And at just the right time, He provided our current building. After experiencing every step in this miraculous journey, I can tell you with confidence that God is in control of every moment of your life. Every single thing that you're waiting, trusting, and believing for—He's already got it all worked out. And guess what? It's going to turn out even better than you're thinking or dreaming today.

Just because we *felt* ready didn't mean we *were* ready. We wanted to get married a year before it was truly time. We wanted to launch our church a year or two before it was truly time. I'm so glad we had people who had gone before us praying for us and giving us wisdom. We thought we were ready, but in reality, we needed more time to prepare for what we were stepping into. Now eleven years into leading our church, I can truly say that slow-cooking our way to becoming pastors prepared us for all the curveballs we encountered in starting something from the ground up and leading our church family through Covid—all while raising our own family.

How do we know if we're ready? I've learned to trust I'm ready to move forward after praying and directly asking God if the timing is right, turning to Scripture and reviewing the promises in His Word, and consulting trusted mentors and friends. There is such wisdom in the advice of respected and trusted role models.

And what do we do if we jump too soon and find ourselves in over our heads? Ask for help, and remember that His grace is more than sufficient. He will always send you guidance when you ask for it. So find rest in knowing that whether you feel prepared or unprepared, your heavenly Father has you and will never fail you.

So, when it comes to timing, we don't need to force it. I'm so glad we didn't rush the dream and move to Dallas two years earlier, because I wouldn't have been ready. Starting a church is real—like, *real*. I didn't know how much faith or strength or backbone I would need for the journey. I didn't realize just how much time I would need to spend on my face crying out to God. So I'm glad we moved when it was God's perfect time.

We're called to give life to powerful things. You know it's true, because God chose a woman to bring Jesus to this earth. He chose a woman because He knew that He could trust her to nurture this promise. What a calling. Yet so many of us women constantly deal with insecurity, doubt, fear, and backbiting. We experience bullying and judgment from other women and from our own internal critics every day. If women could simply remember what we're capable of bringing forth into the world and recall that God picked a woman to bring the Son of God to the earth, I believe that realization would give us power and confidence.

If women remembered what we're capable of bringing forth into the world, it would give us power and confidence.

Sin came into this world through a woman in the Garden of Eden, but Jesus, who saves us from sin, also came into this world through a woman. Meditate on that truth for a moment. I think about those who have made lots of mistakes, myself included. I think about those who feel discounted, forgotten, or as though they can't be used by God. Maybe you think that, because of the choices you've made, God can't work through you to touch someone else, change their life, or make a difference. You'd be wrong, my friend. I had you on my mind as I wrote this chapter.

Here's the deal: He can redeem your past and use it for His glory. You may be reading this and feeling guilty, thinking about how you messed up last night, but God can flip your situation and give you a fresh start right now. Any time, any place. You may be thinking, *I'm going to give up on God. If He doesn't show up, I'm just going to give up.* Right now, I promise you, God can flip your situation around. He can change things before your eyes at exactly the right time. If you're waiting for God to show up, for a sign from Him, these words are that sign!

Our world is full of heaviness. I think about the stories that have been going viral in recent years, especially those of kids who have committed suicide because of bullying. One of them was a ten-year-old girl. She got in a fight with another student at school and was beaten up pretty bad. The fight was recorded and posted on social media, and it went viral. When the little girl saw the video, she couldn't handle the embarrassment and the pressure and she took her own life.

When I heard this story, I kept thinking, *What if she knew that she had the seeds of greatness inside? What if she knew that God had an epic plan for her life? What if the girls around her defended her instead of filming the fight? What if they formed a circle of protection around her?* That's what we're called to do for one another. We're called to save lives. This world is crazy. We've got to get our act together, my friend. We've got to read our Bibles.

We've got to speak the Word of God over one another and over our situations because there are ten-year-old kids watching us.

I'm not saying we could have saved her life, necessarily. What I am saying is that when you know confidently that you have the seeds of greatness planted deep inside you, not much can shake you. Yes, you may cry. Yes, you may grow frustrated. But you keep fighting and you keep going with perseverance, because you know that God has planted greatness within you for such a time as this.

I'm here to tell every one of you reading this book that God isn't finished with your life. He called you to bear His promises in this world and share those promises with others. He called you to plant seeds in hearts, deposit confidence in your community, and unlock dreams in the people you meet. He called you to be a solution to some of the problems we see in this world.

The solutions we need for our world are in seed form within us. So, whatever pressures we may face, whatever conversations we engage in about politics, pain, or the tragedies happening all around us, God calls us to bring life and hope and, wherever possible, a solution. We aren't called to participate in the heaviness or darkness. Rather, we're called to bring peace, encouragement, and strength.

Jesus came into this world "born of a woman," and He plans to do much more through women too! He's not done with me, and He's not done with you. He's just getting started. We are the women that He picked for such a time as this.

Every night before bed, we read Scripture with our kids, pray over them, and speak words of life to them. Our kids are seven, twelve, and eighteen. We've done this since they were born. It's beautiful to see how these words come to pass in their lives. Words are powerful, and when we set aside time to speak life over ourselves and our family and friends, something powerful happens.

One of the things we pray over our kids is our church creed:

> I am loved by God.
> I cannot earn it.
> I cannot lose it.
> In Christ I am forgiven and made brand new.
> I live with passion and purpose.
> I am empowered by the Spirit
> To be the Church in the world
> And to live for the glory of God.[1]

This creed is my prayer for you, and I urge you to make your own version as your personal creed.

We have to get into the rhythm of preaching to ourselves: "I have the peace of God in me. The hope of the world lives in my heart. Yes, the storm may be raging outside, but I'm going to speak life. Everything may feel heavy right now, but I'm going to speak life. The situation may seem hopeless, but I'm going to speak life. I may be experiencing financial tension this month, no one notices the hard work I put into school or my job, my marriage is struggling, but I'm going to keep believing that God is working here. Jesus is with me now."

I can't wait to see what God does in your heart and life.

Isaiah 9 is the perfect response to the times we're all living through:

> Nevertheless, that time of darkness and despair will not go on forever. The land of Zebulun and Naphtali will be humbled, but there will be a time in the future when Galilee of the Gentiles, which lies

along the road that runs between the Jordan and the sea, will be filled with glory.

> The people who walk in darkness
>> will see a great light.
> For those who live in a land of deep darkness,
>> a light will shine.
> You will enlarge the nation of Israel,
>> and its people will rejoice.
> They will rejoice before you
>> as people rejoice at the harvest
>> and like warriors dividing the plunder.
> For you will break the yoke of their slavery
>> and lift the heavy burden from their shoulders.
> You will break the oppressor's rod,
>> just as you did when you destroyed the army of
>>> Midian. . . .

> For a child is born to us,
>> a son is given to us.
> The government will rest on his shoulders.
>> And he will be called:
> Wonderful Counselor, Mighty God,
>> Everlasting Father, Prince of Peace. (verses 1–4, 6)

Wow, doesn't that make you feel so empowered? The situation you're facing today isn't going to last forever. I promise, you're going to come out on the other side.

Your home will be filled with glory. Your neighborhood will be filled with glory. Some of you are surrounded by some serious darkness, and you're trying to be a light for your family and your neighborhood, but Jesus wants to be the light that shines *through* you.

I've been so captivated by the simple line from Galatians 4:4 telling us that Jesus was "born of a woman." Do you feel that call? We are the Marys for this generation.

Take a minute and consider what God has called you to give life to. Maybe He's already given you something to nurture—your career, your family, your neighborhood, a creative project, or a ministry idea. God might be preparing you, revealing ways you can strengthen your skills so that when the time is right, you're ready to partner with Him in bringing light to the world.

You are called for such a time as this!

Remember, God has selected you and I to be alive at this very moment in history. You and I are here for a very real, eternal reason. This moment, this year, is the exact time He has positioned you for greatness. He has set you apart to bring healing to a hurting world. Your story, your example, your perspective, your highs and lows—God can transform them into a powerful road map for others to follow. It's not by accident that He has called you to be on the earth at this appointed time. You're not here by mistake or just to exist. You're here because you bring so much goodness and life; you're here because someone else needs what you have. So hold your head up high, and walk into the next room with confidence, knowing your time is now, the girl is you, and your heavenly Father has called you just like He called so many before you.

Let's Pray ———————————————————————

Jesus, You came into this world born of a woman, so what do You want to bring to life through me? Choose me, God. Pick me, God. Use me to seek and save the lost and to help those in need. Thank You, Lord, that You are almighty God. Thank You that You bring everlasting peace to circumstances, families, and neighborhoods. Thank You for choosing a woman to bring forth the Savior of the world. Would You remind me that Your peace can calm any storm and that You can grow trust and confidence inside me? You know what I'm facing and what I need. May faith and purpose rise up in me. May my heart believe.

2

HONORED BY GOD

We live in a world where some women are constantly tearing one another down, competing, gossiping, and judging. But that's not how we roll as a sisterhood. We encourage; we celebrate; we tell others that they're beautiful and valuable and that God has a plan and purpose for their lives. This is the atmosphere I want us to create in the world, because when we're soaking in encouragement and love, anything is possible. Anything. So let's ignite and stir our faith and expectancy for God to speak to us exactly where we are. He wants to build us up. He wants to make us a city on a hill so that we can be a light in our world.[1] Other women might see us and think, *You're different. You're not judging everyone. You're not gossiping. You just let me come as I am, and you love me right where I am.* First we need to allow Jesus to build us up personally so we can build one another up corporately.

God is the one who is going to make us into the women that

He's called us to be. I've been studying about Jesus, women, and Jesus's heart for women. Women weren't treated well in Jesus's day. They were second-class citizens and couldn't study the Word of God; they weren't always allowed to participate in religious practices.[2] But Jesus flipped the script on all of this. He honored, defended, and spoke up for women. He fought for the woman accused of adultery and protected her from being stoned.[3] He stopped in the middle of a crowd to speak to the woman who had suffered for years from an issue of blood. He knew the moment she touched Him, even in a crowd.[4] He then healed a little girl.[5] He also found a woman in a synagogue, healed her on the Sabbath, which was unheard of, and called her "a daughter of Abraham."[6] I love how He performed many miracles and defended the value of women not just in private locations but also in public.

When Jesus died on the cross and then rose again, He appeared for the first time to women.[7] And guess what? He commissioned women to be evangelists alongside His male disciples.[8]

Jesus talked to the woman at the well, even though in His day Jewish men wouldn't talk to a Samaritan woman. He said to her, "You have had five husbands, and you aren't even married to the man you're living with now" (John 4:18). That startled her because He had accurately read her past and present. Jesus didn't judge her or make her feel guilty for her lifestyle. Instead, He said, "Those who drink the water I give will never be thirsty again" (verse 14). That Samaritan woman then became an evangelist. She returned to her village and told everybody what Jesus had said, so they all wanted to hear Jesus speak.[9]

If you take one thing from this chapter—one thing from this book even—hear this: Jesus is for women. All throughout the

Bible, God was honoring women. He didn't judge the woman who was caught in adultery. He didn't judge her but forgave her and called her to a life of freedom and righteousness.[10]

We serve a God who believes in us and says, "I'm going to lead you by the hand, reveal Myself to you, and then launch you into your purpose, your destiny, and your ministry." This is good news. As I lay the foundation in this chapter, it's important that we understand women's history, and it's important for us to get a different glimpse of Jesus. If you open the Gospels, you'll find so many stories about what He did for women in the Bible and what He still wants to do for us today.

God is continuing to build you up right now by adding layer after layer of His provision and grace. You're built up by the Word of God. You're built up because God believes in you and because you're the head and not the tail, you're above and not beneath.[11] You can do all things through Christ, who strengthens you.[12] You're built up by and for Him. Walk and rest in that truth.

In Luke 6:47–48, Jesus said, "I will show you what it's like when someone comes to me, listens to my teaching, and then follows it. It is like a person building a house who digs deep and lays the foundation on solid rock." That's what we're doing in this chapter—laying the foundation. Of course, many of you know about Jesus, but He is so multifaceted. Whether you've been walking with Him for a long time or you're just starting to give Him a chance, dare to pray, "God, take me deeper. Take me further."

Jesus continued in verse 48, "When the floodwaters rise and break against that house, it stands firm because it is well built." We're going to be well built so that when the floodwaters come, we will stand.

But in verse 49, He warns us, "Anyone who hears and doesn't obey is like a person who builds a house . . . without a foundation. When the floods sweep down against that house, it will collapse into a heap of ruins."

I remember seeing a picture of a house that was still standing after Hurricane Ike wiped out so much territory several years ago. Devastation circled the house, but the structure stood strong. To me, that represents sisterhood and us women united as a force of peace and strength. When storms come, we still stand because our houses are built on the rock of Jesus Christ.

The storms *will* come—life *will* throw us crazy curveballs. Unfortunately, so many women are like houses without firm foundations, so their lives are rubble. But God can rearrange that rubble into a foundation so you can begin anew. He can build your life into something beautiful. You *will* stand the test. You *will* stand the trials. I don't know what thoughts are plaguing you, what's frustrating you, or what's holding you back, but allow God to build a firm foundation, and watch the beautiful things He builds on it. We're going to be women who stand firm. We're going to stand by one another. We're going to stand for one another.

I've been studying about the foundation of houses because Jesus used several analogies about building. I learned that any mistakes made in laying the foundation of a house will compromise the structure if it continues to be built. This phenomenon is known as compounding defects. Laying the foundation correctly is a crucial part of the construction process. So if the foundation of your life isn't built correctly, the more you're promoted, the more doors that open to you, and the more favor that

HONORED BY GOD   19

comes your way, the more your life's construction might be compromised, until it eventually crashes like a deck of cards. But God is laying the foundation of our lives so we will stand the test of time.

A while ago, my girlfriend Kacey and her husband, Ben, were house hunting. They found a brand-new house that was beautiful outside and inside with amazing kitchen countertops. Kacey kept texting me pictures of this house, and everything looked stunning. It was such a good price too. But as they dug deeper, they found that the house had foundation problems. At first, it seemed lovely, but if they had bought it, they would've been forced to make foundation repairs. It's so important to lay the right foundation.

You can hide a faulty foundation for a while, but the cracks will eventually show.

Christ is our rock, our cornerstone. He holds us all together. If we build our lives on Him, we're going to be able to stand taller. When the winds and waves come, we'll still stand because we're standing on the foundation of Christ. "On Christ, the solid Rock, [we] stand: All other ground is sinking sand."[13]

The only foundation that can withstand all storms, all pressures, is Christ.

Your boyfriend isn't your foundation.

Your finances aren't your foundation.

Your job isn't your foundation.

Even your church isn't your foundation.

When the storms come, you'll be able to stand and you'll wonder, *How am I still fighting? How do I have peace when all this crazy stuff is happening?* It's because you're saying, "I'm standing on the Rock. I'm not looking to my husband; I'm not looking to my boyfriend; I'm not looking to how many people think I'm amazing. I'm looking to the One who created me, the One who built me, the One who said, 'I'm going to take a rib from man to create this amazing woman.' This is who I'm standing on."

I think we get so frustrated in life and so discouraged because we're not relying on Christ. Ephesians 2:19–22 tells us, "You *belong* here, with as much right to the name Christian as anyone. God is building a home. He's using us all—irrespective of how we got here—in what he is building. . . . He's using you, fitting you in brick by brick, stone by stone, with Christ Jesus as the cornerstone that holds all the parts together. We see it taking shape day after day—a holy temple built by God, all of us built into it, a temple in which God is quite at home" (MSG).

Christ is our cornerstone and our foundation. He builds us one day at a time.

So, however you feel today, God still wants to use you. Whatever you did last night, God still wants to use you. Whatever you might do tomorrow, God still wants to use you. Regardless of how you got here, you are a part of His grand story.

* * *

It's important for us to remember that it's on God that we build our lives. We put our trust in Him. That way when the storms come, we're going to hold on to Him. We're not going to hold on to that relationship. We're not going to hold on to the things of this world. We're going to grab hold of His hand.

What does that look like practically? It looks like praying for a boyfriend, then getting the boyfriend, but still keeping God first. It looks like praying for a baby or a dream job, then holding a beautiful newborn or receiving wonderful opportunities, but still keeping God first. Many of us are disciplined and locked in until we get what we want. Then, even though we don't mean to, we end up putting the thing we prayed and believed for in front of the One who gave us the gift and made the gift possible. A safeguard could be to ask people you trust to hold you accountable to keep Christ at the center of your life even when you get the thing you've been praying for.

There is a great worship song by Cody Carnes called "Firm Foundation," and a few of the lines go like this:

> Rain came and wind blew
> But my house was built on You . . .
> Yeah, I'm going to make it through
> 'Cause I'm standing strong on You.[14]

I'm hoping that a wildfire will be set off in us. I'm hoping that each one of us will say, "God, I'm going to be in love with You like never before. You're going to be that friend who sticks closer than a brother.[15] You're going to cherish me. You're going to woo me." People give off certain signs when they're in love, and I think it's time for us to show that we're in love with Jesus. Maybe we just talk about Him nonstop, or people ask, "Wow, why are you smiling so much?" We might respond eagerly, excited to talk about Him, just like the woman at the well, who was forever marked by her encounter with Him. The woman with the issue of blood chased after Jesus in the crowd because she knew, *If I just touch Him, I'm going to be healed.* So let's chase Him; let's pursue Him, and let's be desperate for Him in every situation. Let's be like those women who went to Jesus's grave and said, "I'm looking for Him. Where is He?" Whatever we're going through, let's look for Jesus. If our marriage is getting crazy, we look for Jesus. If our job seems unstable, we look for Jesus. If our girlfriends are causing more drama than Mary J. Blige, we look for Jesus.

I'm so sorry for the pain you're carrying. Whatever has been ruined in your life, Jesus can bring it back to life as He lays a new foundation. Let's shine with love when we talk about Him. Let's say to our friends, "I'm going to tell you about a man who will never leave or forsake me. I'm going to tell you about a man who says that I am beautiful, that I am strong, that I am courageous, and that I am brilliant. His name is Jesus."

When we build our lives on Him, like the song says, storms will come. But when we fix our eyes on Jesus and not our "stuff," our perspective has a lot more grit to it, and the weight of our cares are not on our shoulders but on His.

Let's Pray

Dear Jesus, please forgive me for all the times I took You out of the equation. For all the times I said You were first but I didn't walk it out. Please remind me that You are unshakable. Remind me that You remain, even when things don't go according to plan. Remind me that You are my source, my portion, my provider. I commit today to keep You first and to build my life on You.

3

A NEW NAME

When our firstborn son, Parker, was born, I would practice saying his name to hear how it sounded and writing it on paper to see how it looked. I would write "Parker McClellan" over and over on any scrap paper around. I loved how it looked.

We invest so much in naming. We take care to name our children, our businesses, even our cars, right? My husband, Earl, and I named our first car together Hannah. She didn't have any air-conditioning, but she took us so far.

Naming is a sacred act. There's so much power in the naming of objects and people.

Isaiah 62:1–2 reads,

> Because I love Zion,
>> I will not keep still.

Because my heart yearns for Jerusalem,
> I cannot remain silent.

I will not stop praying for her
> until her righteousness shines like the dawn,
> and her salvation blazes like a burning torch.

The nations will see your righteousness.
> World leaders will be blinded by your glory.

And you will be given a new name
> by the LORD's own mouth.

You, my friend, are Zion in this verse. Because God loves you, He will not keep silent. And you will be given a new name straight from the Lord's mouth.

Now listen, I know we're all carrying names right now, and most of them aren't the same ones on our birth certificates. I don't know what labels have been forced on you. But I do know that God has a special, unique, beautiful, and wholly true name for you. Could you stretch your faith today and ask Him to prepare your heart to receive your new name? Because God's not done with you yet. He's working on your situation, on your life, and on you even now.

Maybe you were called hurtful names when you were a child. Bring them to mind now. Derogatory names and harsh comments are damaging, and sometimes we carry them deep within us for years and years.

No matter what names or comments are still in your head from years ago, I can tell you today that God wants to give you a new name. In fact, He gave new names to biblical characters frequently.

God spoke to the father of our faith, Abram, and gave him the new name Abraham.[1] The name Abram means "exalted father." Abraham means "father of many."[2] God essentially said to Abraham, "Not only are you going to be a father, but I'm also going to change the course of your life, and you're going to be a father to many!" And God changed the name of Abraham's wife from the endearing Sarai, meaning "my princess,"[3] to the royal Sarah, meaning "princess."[4] He declared a new vision over their lives and signified it with new names.

A name change is fundamentally a change in God's description of you, a clarification of His vision for your life. It usually means He's changing some part of your life to fulfill His plan. When you get married, earn a PhD, or become a doctor, your name and signature change. In the same way, I want every woman reading this book to finish it with a new signature. You will no longer write what you heard growing up, whether you were called "dumb," "bossy," "ugly," or "not good enough."

Regardless of what labels weigh you down, there is a God in heaven who loves you and knows every aspect of you and your life. And He calls you by your true name.

One label I had to shake free of was the stereotypical idea of a pastor's wife. I don't play the piano, I don't sing, I don't wear dresses every Sunday, and the only hat I wear is a baseball cap. I love expressing myself through fashion. And I decided a long time ago to be committed to being myself even with a lot of eyes on me. People will try to limit you or put you into a certain mold. My pastor and mentor modeled for me that just because you're a pastor doesn't mean you have to force yourself to be something you're not. She taught me to throw away labels and to remember at all times who God says I am.

God changed Abraham's name, calling him a father of many,

before the promise of the name came true. Let that sink in. You may be feeling forgotten or abandoned, but you can't stay there, because God is saying, "You're chosen. You're appointed.[5] I have a plan and purpose for your life."[6]

Sometimes we assume our names can't change until we actually live in a new identity. But God changed Abraham's name and spoke a vision over him long before he was a father of multitudes. Similarly, God can change your name *before* your circumstances change. He sees what we don't see.

Abraham was in his nineties, and God still changed his name. I think about older women who are reading this. Now, I'm an older woman myself. Sometimes I forget that I'm in my forties, because I still feel like I'm in my twenties. So I go up to the young girls at my church, and I'm like, "Hey, girl!" And they say, "I love you so much! You remind me of my mom." I guess I'm not as cool as I thought. But that's okay. My point is, no matter how old you are, now is the perfect time to begin believing and living in the names God gives you.

God isn't done with you. Your story isn't over. He can give you a brand-new name whether you're in your teens or sixties. When we get older, we sometimes think, *I'm done. It's the younger generation's turn.* Instead, be expectant and ask, "God, what's my new name?"

God isn't done with you.

Some of us just get stuck. We get used to our names and labels. But God is calling us to step out of our comfort zone. He's calling us to step out in faith. You might hear,

You're fat.

You're never going to amount to anything.

You'll always be depressed.

Your circumstance is never going to change.

You're useless.

But God is bigger than those labels. He says,

None of those labels define you.

That lie is not your name.

I have given you a true name.

You are My chosen daughter.

I have a plan and purpose for your life.

Maybe our circumstances haven't changed, but He is bigger than our circumstances. He is bigger than our thoughts. He is bigger than our wildest dreams. Jesus is everything. He has given us brand-new names. Sometimes we have to step out in faith and trust that God is changing us even though nothing changes in our situations.

Let me say that again: We have to trust that God is growing us even when our situations haven't changed.

If you're lonely, call yourself accepted, believed in, and loved. If you feel worn out, confess that "the joy of the Lord is your strength" (Nehemiah 8:10). When you feel weak, confess that "[you] can do everything through Christ, who gives [you] strength" (Philippians 4:13).

Sometimes we just replay those old labels like a broken record. Our thoughts try to hold us captive so we'll become enslaved to them. But God wants to bring us freedom.

In Rome, slaves had a single name and when a slave was freed, they usually kept their slave name and adopted their former owner's name. For example, a Roman inscription tells us that a man named Publius Larcius freed a male slave who was then called Publius Larcius Nicia.[7] The freed slave kept his slave name even though he had a new name. Sometimes, when God is trying to give us a brand-new name, we just add our slave name to it instead of walking in our free name. I've seen women freed from unhealthy habits and even abuse but years later, they still cling to the familiarity of old mindsets. Though God gives us freedom and new life, sometimes we merely add our slave name onto our new name. But today, let God set you totally and completely free.

> *Don't hang on to your slave name instead of walking in your free name.*

The lies and labels of the Enemy might be plaguing our minds, holding us back from living freely as the women God created us to be. But God is saying, "You know what? I'm pressing stop on those lies. I'm giving you a brand-new name." He's erasing those labels, those lies, that enslave us. He's saying, "My daughter, I know you, and from heaven, I'm bestowing on you a brand-new name."

Maybe you've been a slave to your old thoughts, old ways of living, old circumstances, or old mindsets. God is ready to fill your heart with freedom and truth. Right now, you're going from slave to free.

Without knowing it, some of us have put ourselves—and God—in a box. We come to believe, *Oh, I'm just a student* or *I'm just a mom*. But God is saying, "You are more than that. I have a plan and a purpose for you on your college campus. I want you to tell people about Me. I have a plan and a purpose for you as a stay-at-home mom that extends beyond giving out little goldfish crackers at the park. I want you to own this season and put to use all the gifts and talents I've given you."

Our God is expansive. And where culture shoves us into tight roles and claustrophobic identities, He calls us to expand our mindset, take up space, and live fully as our whole selves.

But I'll let you in on a powerful truth: It's not just about you. When we embrace our God-given names and own our God-given identity, we encourage those around us to do the same.

A single stroke of President Abraham Lincoln's pen on the Emancipation Proclamation changed the legal status of three million enslaved people in America and eventually led to the liberation of all slaves.[8] Where God's spirit is, there is freedom.[9] His freedom is with you where you are right now. His freedom is about to fill you like never before. And your freedom will help bring others into freedom too.

God has called us each by name, and what beautiful names they are. I want to urge you to open your heart now for a minute, and as you read the names that God calls you, I really hope you'll slow down and let them settle deep into your identity. This is how the God of the universe sees you:

Saved[10]
Righteous[11]
The Light of the World[12]

Redeemed[13]

Loved[14]

Chosen[15]

Overcomer[16]

Daughter of God[17]

These are just a few of the incredible names God has given you. Read that list again, and consider which of these true names feel easy for you to carry and which feel like they don't quite fit. Bring the ones that don't quite fit yet to the Lord, and ask Him to help you believe His words until they become part of who you are.

Now the old names probably won't disappear when you turn the last page of this chapter. I wish they would! Renewing our minds and our identities can take time. But when you find yourself slipping back into old ways of thinking about yourself, speak your true names over and over until the old names lose power.

If we've believed lies about ourselves for too long, it can feel uncomfortable to let them go. Let me assure you, God wants you to know that He loves you and that He hasn't forgotten about you. I want you to think about whatever you're holding tightly to, whatever you won't surrender, whatever names you think you can't or God can't change. I just want you to relax. I want you to open your hands and open your heart and say, "God, take anything from me that isn't like You. Take away whatever is trying to bind me. I want to become free, because Christ came to set me free."[18]

I'm believing that God is going to take those names and lies that have tried to enslave you and that He's going to fill your heart with freedom.

Let's Pray ————————————————

Before you pray, visualize your Savior removing burdens from your back. Ask Jesus to give you a mental picture.

Dear Jesus, thank You for lifting off every burden I am carrying this very moment. Please let Your grace and ease fall fresh on me. I declare that no weapon formed against me shall prosper and that in You I am healed and whole. Thank You that You have given me, Your daughter, a new name and replaced the old. I will now answer by my new name and not respond when my old name is called. Purify my heart, renew my mind, and set me free. In Jesus's name, amen.

4

DAUGHTER OF THE KING

Every year, our church hosts a women's conference called Cultivate. Basically, we throw a party for women in Dallas and all over the world to show them that we love them and believe in them. We pray all year long for God to move supernaturally in breakthroughs at the conference. One year we dedicated the entire conference to talking about what it means to be God's daughter, because when you realize that you're God's daughter, every label, every doubt, and every fear gets erased. It's so freeing to walk in that confidence, knowing our Father's got it. He's just got it. We can walk into a room with our heads held high because God, our Father, is the King. He's our provider and protector. He's in control. We can walk confidently into any number of stressful situations with that truth in our hearts.

We are royal. We belong to the King. First Peter 2:9–10 says, "You are the ones chosen by God, chosen for the high calling of priestly work, chosen to be a holy people, God's instruments to do his work and speak out for him, to tell others of the night-and-day difference he made for you—from nothing to something, from rejected to accepted" (MSG). That's good news! You might feel like you're nothing, but I'm believing that by the time we finish this chapter, God is going to wake up your gifting. You don't have to walk around in this world feeling rejected, because that's not true—*you belong.*

That's what our lives are about: to make known His perfections, even when we feel weak. God blesses us when we lead people to Him despite our weakness. When we're stretched, we know that we're going to get to the other side of the stretching because He's working in our lives to tell His story.

You're God's heavenly daughter whom He loves and brags about.

I imagine He has His own photo album up in heaven and shows all the angels pictures of His daughters, saying, "Oh, look at her hair. It's getting long because she's growing it out. Go, girl—you're looking good. Oh, she got a weave? I like that. Look how she brilliantly navigated that situation. I'm so proud. Look how she showed up when it was hard. She's so strong." I'm sure He's up there just bragging on His girls because He's proud of us. He wants you to know that you're royalty because you're with Him.

You can walk into any room with confidence, saying, "You know what? I'm with Him. I'm royal and I'm His daughter."

Let's talk about what it means to be a royal daughter.

As royal daughters, we stand strong. It's important for us to walk with confidence and be servants as we wear the crown. We're not royal daughters who walk into the room and say, "Oh, I'm royal. I can't come early and set up." Being royal means we have a responsibility. We're the chief servants. That's what I love about women serving in the church, in our communities, in our families and workplaces. We're not afraid to get our hands dirty. We come early, we stay late, we sign up to volunteer, and we text and encourage one another. God is calling us to that mission. He entrusts us with this important work because it's not about us— we're about one another, and He's about us. As we wear these proverbial crowns, know that they come from Christ and that we're called to follow Him in servanthood.

Scripture gives us a look at two royal daughters. The first is Esther.[1]

Esther was a Jewish orphan in Persia who had been adopted by her older cousin Mordecai. King Xerxes had grown dissatisfied with his queen and ordered the beautiful young women of each province to be brought, willingly or not, to the palace as candidates for his new queen. Esther was one of those young women. While she was in the palace, she followed all the orders and didn't ask for much. I don't know how long I would have been able to survive in that palace, because I like my coffee and my bottled water. Don't judge me, but I'm picky when it comes to those things, and that's okay because we all have our quirks. But Esther didn't ask for anything extra. She did what the assistant said.

By the end of the preparation period, Esther was the most

admired woman in the palace, and the king noticed her and crowned her the new queen.

While Esther was still getting used to wearing a crown, the king gave his buddy Haman a promotion. Have you ever seen someone receive a position of leadership and start acting differently? This guy started acting crazy, walking around and demanding, "Kiss my ring. I've got plans. I'm next to the king." Haman just started acting the fool. (This is the Oneka paraphrase, of course.)

But Mordecai, who worked in the palace, said, "I'm not bowing down. I'm not bowing down to anyone."

Then Haman got mad. "You know what I'm going to do? I'm going to annihilate all the Jews. I'm going to have the king sign this little edict, and before you know it, the Jews are going to be gone."

Mordecai ripped his clothes in grief, put on burlap rags, and started doing the ugly cry outside the palace. Word got to Esther. People told her, "Your relative is breaking down." Doesn't this sound like a movie?

Esther sent her assistant to Mordecai to ask what happened, and Mordecai explained the situation: "Our people are going to be killed, and you, Esther, need to do something about it. You need to talk to that king who thinks you're the most beautiful woman in the world. You need to use his favor to rescue us. You are an appointed royal daughter."

Esther said, "If I go talk to the king, I might be executed because you can talk to the king only when you've been invited into his court. I haven't received an invitation in thirty days."

Mordecai then reminded her of her calling: "You have been chosen as a royal daughter for such a time as this."

Isn't *calling* a good word? You've been called to your job. You've been called to your family. You've been called to your school to raise up girls for such a time as this.

In my imagination, I see Esther get a little gangster. She tilted her crown and said, "If I die, I die" (Esther 4:16, MSG). And that part's not paraphrased. She went from "I can't approach the king, because I could lose my life" to "If I die, I die."

That fight was in her.

Esther put on her royal robe and walked into the throne room, and the king extended his scepter and said, "What do you want, girl? You can have up to half the kingdom." Esther soon set a clever plan in motion and saved her people. Now that's what I call a royal daughter. She trusted God, had confidence in her calling, and advocated for others.

Then there's another royal daughter who was a little bit of a hot mess.

In Mark 6:17–28, we read the story of John the Baptist. He had told the ruler Herod, "It's against God's will for you to marry your brother's wife, Herodias." Herodias was married, then left her husband for his brother. Because of John's stance, Herodias wanted to kill him. She thought, *How can John tell me that my marriage isn't right?*

She was offended and nurtured a grudge. Women are nurturers by nature, and we can sometimes nurture the wrong things. That's what Herodias did—she nurtured that grudge until she birthed the idea to have John the Baptist killed. But without Herod's approval, she was powerless. Herod respected and feared John, a holy man, so he was stuck in inaction.

Mark tells us, "Herodias's chance finally came on Herod's birthday. He gave a party for his high government officials, army officers, and the leading citizens of Galilee" (verse 21). Herodias, the queen, told her daughter, "I want you to dance for your stepdad."

Salome[2] performed a dance, maybe something like a dance from Beyoncé's Renaissance tour, and Herod was so pleased that, just like the king in Esther's story, he said, "Ask me for anything. You can have anything you like." That was her moment of truth. It was just like when the king offered Esther half his kingdom. Esther then used that power to save her people. I thought it was so fascinating that both royal women were given the same opportunity.

Salome asked her mother, "Mom, what should I ask for?" Because Herodias was holding a grudge, she said, "Ask for the head of John the Baptist!" (verse 24). So Salome hurried back to Herod and told him, "I want the head of John the Baptist, right now, on a tray!" (verse 25). John the Baptist—this man who was setting the course for Jesus, baptizing people, and embracing the Spirit of God—his life was suddenly taken because someone bore a grudge, using her royal position for evil. The king regretted his pledge, but because he had made it in front of his party guests, he couldn't say no. So he sent an executioner to John the Baptist's cell, and his head was placed on a platter.

Two royal daughters—one who used her platform and crown to set captives free and one who used her crown for destruction and annihilation. One royal daughter tried to protect others, and the other tried to protect herself.

God has given us crowns in the Spirit, and we can use them to build one another up, to build marriages, to build families, and to build our careers, or we can use them to tear down and bring destruction. If we're honest, many of us have used our platforms or voices to manipulate and bring about situations that serve only ourselves. I want you to know that God is a redeemer and

He can take you from a Herodias or Salome to an Esther in a second.

Herodias was called to be a hero. It's right in her name.[3] She came from a priestly family, but she didn't live her calling to be a royal daughter. Her daughter's name, Salome, means "peace."[4] She was supposed to bring peace to every situation. So you have this mother-daughter duo who had unparalleled potential to be heroes and peace-givers for the kingdom, but instead they brought destruction.

God has given you a platform and a calling. He wants you to use all your influence, your hard work, and your words for good and for His glory. I just want you to know that even if you feel overwhelmed by mistakes you've made or if you've been nurturing a grudge, God can restore your life in a second.

Years ago, when I was in college the first time around—yes, I went to college twice. Hey, what? I went to undergrad for seven years. I was a hot mess the first go-around. I started partying and craving boys' attention. I made a lot of very bad choices with men. After living this life for a while, I said, "You know what? I'm going to give my life to Christ." The Bible says, "Old things have passed away; behold, all things have become new" (2 Corinthians 5:17, NKJV). Something new came over me, and I began believing, *I'm valuable. I'm worth more than this. God has someone special for me.* I wish I could've just been patient and not tried to pick out my husband by myself, because my only criteria were that he be handsome and believe in God, but that's a wide range. I got myself into trouble with men that were handsome and just believed in God a little. I finally realized who I was in Christ and said to myself, *I'm not going to settle. I'm going to be single as long as it takes.*

I was using my crown negatively, but then I learned my value in

Christ. And I ended up meeting my husband, Earl, who is my very best friend and, besides Jesus, the best thing that has ever happened to me. I've never met another human like him. I can start crying talking about him.

I met Earl when we were in college. One day he finally asked me out. We were just talking and hit it off. We became best friends; then we started dating, our relationship got serious, and we started sharing our stories.

Earl gave his life to the Lord at seven years old. His mother is awesome, and he was raised in a Christian home. He wasn't perfect, but he basically walked the straight and narrow. When he met me, I was just three years into living for Christ. But because God's light was shining through me and He had redeemed me, old things were passed away and Earl didn't see my past. I'm glad he didn't. I'm glad social media wasn't present back then, because he would've looked me up and run.

One morning we went to breakfast in our school cafeteria and just started telling each other our stories. I was dreading this part, because when you fall in love with someone, you don't want to have a past anymore. When I was out there just being my own woman and doing what I wanted, hanging out with who I wanted, and making all those poor choices, there was a rush. I thought, *I'm independent. I'm in control. My body is mine, and I can do what I want.* But when I looked into the eyes of the person that I'd prayed for, who for so long I didn't even think I deserved, I wished that I didn't have a past. Earl saved himself for marriage, so I felt like he needed to know my story. After I told him, I left breakfast thinking, *I wonder what he thinks about me. I wonder if he's still going to value me. Even though he's a Christian, I just wonder what he's thinking.*

The next morning, we met again for breakfast and he brought me a white rose. I'll never forget that. Earl said, "I want you to know that you're the purest girl I know and the purest girl I've ever met in my life."

I just want to tell you, girl—there is power and redemption in the blood of Jesus Christ. God used Earl to tell me that He saw me as pure, just as He sees you as pure. Whether you've lived like Esther and know how to rock your crown or you've lived like Herodias and Salome and didn't have pure motives, I want you to know that God is a redeemer and a restorer. God sees you as His royal, beautiful, spotless daughter.

> *God sees you as His royal, beautiful, spotless daughter.*

No matter how many mistakes you've made, no matter the fears that plague your mind, God says, "Even in the midst of your mess, I'm bigger than it all. I want you to see Me through My blood that I shed for you on the cross. I want you to see yourself as free. I want you to see yourself as whole. I want you to see yourself as redeemed and restored, and complete. I want you to see yourself standing strong like a tower, wearing your crown, walking with authority, walking with boldness, walking with My presence, and walking with purpose."

"The King's daughter is all glorious within" (Psalm 45:13, NASB).

God is making you glorious within. He's renewing you. He's restoring you. Right now, God is saying, "You are My royal daughter. You are My princess. You are from a royal priesthood, a chosen generation.[5] I have a plan and a purpose for your life. I will not abandon you like others have in the past. You're not rejected.[6] You're accepted. I bought you with a price.[7] I shed My blood to remind you that you have dignity, that you have courage, that you are brave, that you are strong, and that you are being perfected." Let's make this our confession and prayer:

> As royal daughters, we build up; we don't break down.
> We plant; we don't uproot.
> We speak life, not death.
> We see the best, not the worst.
> We put back together; we don't tear apart.
> Lord, may we walk in the integrity of our place as royal
> daughters today and every day.

Let's Pray

> Dear Jesus, help me see myself the way You see me.
>
> Thank You for reminding me that I am Your daughter.
>
> Thank You that I'm adopted by You and clothed in royal
>
> garments. Help me not settle or see myself the way the
>
> world sees me. May I be defined by Your love and the

strength, grace, and honor that You have bestowed on me. May I walk into every room, meeting, and encounter standing tall, knowing You walk with me and before me. I'm called, chosen, and set apart by You. Thank You for calling me for such a time as this.

5

BIRTHRIGHT OF PEACE

We all need more peace in our lives. And the war for peace starts in our minds.

Children sometimes have night terrors. Have you ever heard of those? A child wakes up from one, and they're not just scared; they're terrified. Some of us have mind terrors all the time—day or night. These mind terrors distract us and divert our course. But in this chapter, I'm going to unpack how to attain the perfect peace that surpasses all understanding and guards our hearts and our minds in Christ Jesus.[1]

Galatians 5:22–23 says, "The Holy Spirit produces this kind of fruit in our lives: love, joy, peace, patience, kindness, goodness, faithfulness, gentleness, and self-control." Circumstances attempt to steal our peace, joy, and rest. In our day, we can't drive in traffic, stand in line at a store, or shop online without losing our peace.

I've studied peace before and prayed it over myself, but I don't know if I've ever taken time to peel back its layers. I feel like I've spent my whole forty-something years trying to arrange my life just right to make it peaceful, but peace can't be manufactured. Peace comes from Christ and from Christ being with us. You can be in the middle of a storm and still have peace because Christ is with you. You can be fighting a battle and still have peace because Christ is with you. You can face debt from school loans and still have peace because Christ is with you. Stop waiting for your circumstances to change. Yes, God has a plan and purpose for your life and situation, but don't wait to have peace until things seem to come together. We need peace even when our situation remains the same. That thought really convicted me. I've been trying to create peace my whole life when it's been available the whole time.

God wants to teach us to recognize peace. Second Corinthians 4:8 says, "We are pressed on every side by troubles, but we are not crushed. We are perplexed, but not driven to despair." Trials will come. You're probably in a trial or have family or friends that are facing a trial, but you can still have peace until your situation changes. Isn't that the best news? You don't have to wait until the breakthrough; peace can be your breakthrough. You can be alone but not feel alone.

The Bible tells how Jesus is our Prince of Peace. Isaiah prophesied, "To us a child is born, to us a son is given; and the government shall be upon his shoulder." Isaiah was prophesying Jesus's birth here. He continued, "His name shall be called Wonderful Counselor, Mighty God, Everlasting Father, Prince of Peace" (Isaiah 9:6, ESV). He's our Wonderful Counselor. Whatever weight we're carrying isn't too heavy for Him, because He's our Mighty

God, our Everlasting Father, and our Prince of Peace. Here's the deal: Jesus is with you. He loves you. "He will never leave you nor forsake you" (Deuteronomy 31:8, NIV). He wants to hold your hand through whatever storm you're facing. He wants to teach you to recognize His peace and His presence. He struggled through storms. People betrayed Him. But He still had peace in the midst of life.

I've spent too much time waiting for life to all line up correctly. I want to learn how to be peaceful when life is chaotic, because we live in the real world.

Peace is so different from just stillness, calmness, and quiet. Look at this biblical definition of *peace:* "the joining or binding together of what has been broken, divided, or separated."[2] Meditate on that for a second. "The joining together of broken parts" is the biblical definition of *peace.*

> Peace *means "the joining together of that* what *has been divided."*

Certain life situations hijack our peace, and the pressures of life constantly attack it. I want to alert you to some attitudes, mindsets, and circumstances that are trying to steal your peace.

Abandonment

So many of us have felt abandoned or have actually been abandoned. Maybe a boyfriend unexpectedly broke up with you. Maybe a husband cheated on you. Maybe a family member walked out on you. Maybe a friend deserted you. Jesus also knows what it feels like to be abandoned. His disciples, His friends, deserted Him right as He needed their presence the most. So He knows how it feels to be forgotten. He knows how it feels to be left. He knows how it feels to not be valued. One of the many reasons I wrote this book is that I want every woman—no matter her size, her situation, or her skin color—to know she is loved, valued, and believed in because she has a Savior who died on the cross for her.

Jesus talked to His friends and said, "Do you finally believe? In fact, you're about to make a run for it—saving your own skins and abandoning me. But I'm not abandoned. The Father is with me" (John 16:31–32, MSG). So even if you've been walked out on, you're not abandoned. Even if your family doesn't talk to you, you're not abandoned. Jesus continued, "I've told you all this so that trusting me, you will be unshakable and assured, deeply at peace" (verse 33, MSG). When those lies come your way, remind yourself that you haven't been abandoned, because your Father is right there with you.

As I was working on this chapter, I had to examine my own heart and ask, "Do I have an issue with the spirit of abandonment?" I want to tell you a little piece of my story. My mom and dad fell in love, and I was born, but my dad was in college on a track scholarship and decided to abandon his post as a father to finish school. So my mom raised me by herself. When I was growing up, I don't remember asking, "Where's my dad? Why is my dad not around?" My mom covered for him really well, but as I got older, I would go to weddings and see fathers give their daughters away. That's when I realized what I had been missing out on, but I just kind of went along with my life.

My uncle Fred, who acted as a father figure to me, actually gave me away at my wedding, but now he's in heaven. I first felt abandoned when he passed away from cancer, because he covered for my father like my mom did. Suddenly, I didn't feel safe anymore. The truth about abandonment that I studied for this chapter brought me freedom because I realized I'm not alone. Christ is always with me. He never left. He just wants me to learn to recognize Him. Sometimes you go through life, and the full impact of the trouble that you've faced doesn't hit you until something specific happens. Until my uncle Fred died, I didn't fully realize how abandoned I felt. Even now I take it really hard when a male friend lets me down, but God is working on me. I thought I was free from the sense of abandonment, but as I studied, a whole new layer of freedom was added to the freedom I already had. The good news is that even when all that crazy stuff was happening through my childhood and adulthood, God was always there and His grace has been so sufficient.[3]

Comparison

I want to change the way women do relationships. No gossiping. No backbiting. Only celebration. We as a sisterhood celebrate women who are a size two or forty-two. We celebrate the girls who might not have curves. We celebrate every single woman, no matter her season or her circumstances. We love all the girls in our worlds. We value them and we believe in them. This attitude isn't the norm every place you go. You sometimes don't feel that sense of encouragement and companionship when you go into stores. You sometimes don't feel it at the gym. You sometimes don't feel it at work. That's why it's so important that every girl reading this grasps the heart of what sisterhood is. You might not have ever seen or experienced healthy girl relationships, but God is writing on your heart what sisterhood really means: a girl gang who has your back, who's praying for you, who's cheering you on, and who believes in you.

Perfectionism and comparison—these modes of thinking will steal your peace and your joy. I'm going to be your mentor for a second and tell you to stop comparing yourself with others. You're beautiful exactly how you are. You're beautiful. Stop trying to be perfect. So many of us are killing ourselves trying to be perfect, and that striving is hijacking our peace. You don't have to be perfect. There's only one perfect person, and His name is Jesus Christ. We can't measure ourselves against our friends on social media, because it isn't real. Most people, including me, take twenty pictures before they find the one they use. We all do it, so you can't base what you think about families, kids, parenting, or exercise on social media posts. That can't be your Bible. Yes, you can get inspired. Social media can be an awesome tool, but don't let it be your mirror or your guide. Take the pressure off yourself. Just take a deep breath because no perfect mom, perfect student, perfect single person, or perfect girlboss exists. Nobody's perfect. I'm far from perfect. We all have our crazy days. We all sometimes say things we wish we didn't say. As much as I am in love with my husband, my marriage isn't perfect. Sometimes we get on each other's nerves because we're human, but we're quick to apologize.

Just know that there's no standard here except to fall more in love with Jesus. Then as you fall more in love with Him, He peels off the spirit of perfectionism and comparison.

Fear and Overthinking

These mindsets will try to paralyze you and rob you of peace. The following are some scriptures for those of us who are dealing with fear and anxiety.

Psalm 94:19 comforts me: "When anxiety was great within me, your consolation brought me joy" (NIV).

You may struggle with overthinking or with anxious thoughts. I know I have. It's important to remember where our peace comes from. John 14:27 reminds us, "Peace I leave with you; my peace I give you. I do not give to you as the world gives. Do not let your hearts be troubled and do not be afraid" (NIV).

Philippians 4:6 says, "Don't worry about anything; instead, pray about everything. Tell God what you need, and thank him for all he has done." Sometimes when you're in a funk, you need to stop and remember what you're thankful for; "then you will experience God's peace, which exceeds anything we can understand" (verse 7). I'm praying that God's peace will guard the heart, mind, and life in Christ Jesus of every woman reading this.[4] I want you to pray this prayer for the girls in your world too.

Ephesians 2:13–14 says, "Now in Christ Jesus you who once were far away have been brought near by the blood of Christ. For he himself is our peace" (NIV). Don't look for peace in your circumstances. Because they change, you might feel like you don't have peace often. All hell can be breaking loose around you, but peace comes from within because its source is "Christ in you, the hope of glory" (Colossians 1:27, NIV). Peace is with you because He is with you.

> *Even though peace is our birth-right, in this broken world we have to work to keep our peace.*

We have to work diligently to keep our peace. Psalm 34:14 instructs us, "Turn away from evil and do good. Search for peace, and work to maintain it." You must be aggressive. Gray roots are starting to show around my crown, so I have to work to maintain all this black hair by dyeing my roots. I choose to maintain my hair; I know I don't have to, because gray is gorgeous. My mother-in-law's hair is gray, and she looks fierce. But it's not the right time for me yet, so I have to fight against the gray. To continue to recognize peace, we have to spiritually maintain our hearts and our lives in the same way.

If you want to stay peaceful, you can't just watch anything, do anything, or put yourself in any situation to stay peaceful. You have to work to maintain it. For example, if you're in a season when you're feeling overwhelmed or anxious, it's probably not the best time to watch a movie that is going to give you nightmares or put you on edge. If you're walking through a breakup, it's probably not the best idea to look at old photos. If you're fighting body-image issues, it's probably not wise to scroll through friends' and influencers' Instagram and compare yourself with them. Let's set ourselves up to win and not make it harder on ourselves.

I'm committed to fighting for peace. During the pandemic when our world was turned upside down, it felt like peace was nowhere to be found. Even in our marriage, there were days when my husband wasn't himself and I had to be the bigger person and vice versa. We were leading our church through what felt like hell on earth, homeschooling our kids, protecting our family's health, and dealing with financial pressures, just to name a few challenges. On days when I knew I had reached my limit and couldn't find peace anywhere, I would take a shower, blast worship music, and cry out to God.

It was in my fatigue that I would center my soul and fix my gaze on "the author and perfecter of [my] faith" (Hebrews 12:2, BSB). Those moments weren't a magic wand, but they were a healing balm that would help flood my soul and spirit with an unshakable peace that sent fear and discouragement out the door.

Fighting for peace is done in the little, practical things. Here are a few ideas:

- *Screenshot the prayer below, print it out, and place it somewhere you'll see it often to keep this prayer alive in your soul.*
- *Do the same with any of the comforting scriptures included in this chapter.*
- *Read God's Word.*
- *Get involved in a healthy church.*
- *Find a good therapist or counselor.*
- *Make a habit of writing gratitude lists.*
- *Mentor someone younger than you.*

I hope these ideas help some of you reading this, because you're not alone. So many of us have to fight anxiety and fear in different ways each day. But my hope for all of us is that we recognize and know that peace is with us, has never left us, and will help and comfort us all the days of our lives.

Love peace. Learn to celebrate it. May we be women who love peace and avoid drama. May we be women who speak life, who strengthen one another, and who encourage one another. May we be women who build up and don't tear down. May we be peace-makers.

We need to wear peace. Do you love shoes as much as I do? I love all kinds of shoes. I'm going through an ankle-boot phase currently, but I still love all shoes. Ephesians 6:15 says, "For shoes, put on the peace that comes from the Good News so that you will be fully prepared." This means that we should keep our shoes of peace on every single day. Most of us don't walk around barefooted when we leave the house, so think of putting on peace in the same manner. I want us to comprehend deeper levels of peace and learn to maintain it, because God needs us as His daughters to live above circumstances so we can see things change around us. Because here's the deal: Life is so unpredictable. But if we can learn to navigate life even when it doesn't turn out the way we planned, then we can learn to recognize that peace is with us and has never left us. His name is Jesus Christ. He loves you, He adores you, He believes in you, and He has a plan and a purpose for your life.

I feel like God has been saying, "I've been here all along. I have never left you and I have never forsaken you. I'm so sorry for the bad things that happened to you. I'm so sorry for the hurtful words that were spoken over your life. But old things have passed away, and all things have become new."[5] I'm believing that God is renewing your mind in this moment, that He's performing heart surgery on you, and that your broken heart is being mended, strengthened, encouraged, and made whole.

My prayer is this: "God, whatever abandonment issues I have, break them off. Even if I don't know that they're there. Break off whatever fears and anxieties I have in the name of Jesus." So I'm going first. I'm jumping in. Are you going to jump in with me? The water may be cold, your hair may get wet, but God is with you wherever you are. He wants to pour out His peace and His grace on you like never before. He wants to bless you with "rivers of living water" (John 7:38).

Let's Pray

Lord, You see my fear and anxiety, the abandonment and loneliness. I know You are healing me, and I thank You for continuing to break these chains. You are my Father, the one who never leaves and who is greater and more powerful than all things. Set me free from the thoughts, lies, and insecurities that hold me back, and help me leave them behind for good. Help me fully believe and live in Your peace, because You, Jesus, the Prince of Peace, the King of kings, and the Lord of lords, have made me free.

6

MADE FOR VICTORY

Deborah was a queen bee. She was the only female judge that we have biblical record of. She was one of the few judges to whom the title "prophet" was also given.[1]

Her name means "bee," like a bumblebee.[2] I thought, *You know what? Beyoncé wasn't the first queen bee. Maybe she borrowed that title from Deborah.* Deborah was "a sting for foes, and honey for friends."[3] We want to be a sting to the Enemy and honey for the women in our world, right? Isn't that so good?

Deborah was the original queen bee, and bees are responsible. One-third of our food supply depends on animal pollination of plants, in which bees play a major role.[4] Deborah fulfilled an active and vital role in bringing life to her community, just like a bee. Queen bees let off this fragrance, this aroma, which is a signal for all the bees to unite and work together at whichever tasks are before them.[5] What fragrance do our lives give off? Is the aroma of our lives sweet? Since we are royal daughters, we want to give off an aroma that promotes unity among this generation of women. This is so powerful.

The queen bee is the heart and soul of the beehive. The colony can't survive without her. And that's true for us as women—we are the heart and soul of this world, and the world really can't survive without us.

We are called to bring life to our communities.

Judges 4:1–8 tells her story:

After Ehud's death, the Israelites again did evil in the LORD's sight. So the LORD turned them over to King Jabin of Hazor, a Canaanite king. The commander of his army was Sisera, who lived in Harosheth-haggoyim. Sisera, who had 900 iron chariots, ruthlessly oppressed the Israelites for twenty years. Then the people of Israel cried out to the LORD for help.

Deborah, the wife of Lappidoth, was a prophet who was judging Israel at that time. She would sit under the Palm of Deborah, between Ramah and Bethel in the hill country of Ephraim, and the Israelites would go to her for judgment. One day she sent for Barak son of Abinoam, who lived in Kedesh in the land of Naphtali. She said to him, "This is what the LORD, the God of Israel, commands you: Call out 10,000 warriors from the tribes of Naphtali and Zebulun at Mount Tabor. And I will call out Sisera, commander of Jabin's army, along with his chariots and warriors, to the Kishon River. There I will give you victory over him."

Barak told her, "I will go, but only if you go with me."

Deborah had her judgment seat in the open air, under the shadow of that tree, which was an emblem of justice. I love that she chose a palm to sit under. They can withstand crazy storms; they bend but rarely break under pressure.

She shows us that what we sit under is critical.

What are we sitting under? Instagram, the news, fear, gossip, or what other people think? I love how Deborah sat out in the air and sunshine, not hidden away in the shadows.

Deborah went out to the battlefield. She didn't stay on the sidelines. I love that she was in the field! Deborah and ten thousand warriors against the enemy. That was one courageous girl! Think about it. A woman on the front lines. The insecurity that she had to break through, the barriers and preconceived ideas that they may have had about her.

She carried God's word to the Israelites, who were oppressed. I wonder what problems you carry answers to. That's a question to pray about: "God, what problems are You going to bring solutions to through my life?"

Deborah didn't do it alone. She had help from Jael. Who are you leaning on to help you in the battles you're facing? Sometimes we believe the lie that asking for help is a sign of weakness, but it's a sign of strength.

Deborah must have been tough; she wasn't weak and high-maintenance. I love hotels with air-conditioning, and I'm not the best camper. Don't judge me, because we all have our tolerance levels. But hey, when I'm on the mission field, I can get down and dirty without air-conditioning and water, and I can love on people big-time. When I can choose, though, I choose air-conditioning. But Deborah wasn't high-maintenance. She went on that battlefield, just walking tall among ten thousand warriors. Can you imagine that? An army with nine hundred chariots was facing her, and she was just walking and leading, standing strong and letting off a fragrance of unity. Deborah was confident. She knew who she was and she led boldly. I love that. I've been meditating on the fact that Deborah was found in the field. She found victory by being in the field, not staying at home under her tree.

Before there was any sign of victory, Deborah also prophesied to Barak that the victory was coming. Sometimes we have to speak life into a situation before victory comes. That's what Deborah did. She had to fan the flame of hope within Barak, and she had to prophesy life into a dead situation by believing God for victory. And the victory came.

Deborah faced the battle unafraid. She helped bring strength and strategy to Barak. God gave her a battle plan, and speaking on God's behalf, she said, "This is what you're going to do—you're going to gather the troops, and you're about to wreck shop to get the victory." She had a plan and a purpose. Deborah was soft but strong; she was tough yet tender. And that's okay for women. For my hardcore sisters out there who are like, "I'm rough and tough. I don't like high heels; I wear tennis shoes"—you still have a tender side that God has placed within you to be a strength to other people. You can be tough and tender. You can be strong and kick butt, but you can also be soft, speaking words of life and peace as Deborah did.

The battle raged, and Deborah helped bring the victory by

being God's mouthpiece. But she didn't accomplish the task herself. In the same way, we work better within community, and we aren't called to do life alone.

Another key character in this story is a woman named Jael. The army of ten thousand beat Sisera's army, but Sisera got away on foot. Judges 4:17–18 says, "Sisera ran to the tent of Jael, the wife of Heber the Kenite, because Heber's family was on friendly terms with King Jabin of Hazor. Jael went out to meet Sisera and said to him, 'Come into my tent, sir.'"

"Please give me some water," Sisera said. "I'm thirsty" (verse 19). So Jael gave him some milk. Then he said to her, "Stand at the door of the tent. If anybody comes and asks you if there is anyone here, say no" (verse 20). The battle had just finished. Sisera was in her tent, and Jael had a plan of action. "When Sisera fell asleep from exhaustion, Jael quietly crept up to him" (verse 21). I love when biblical stories come alive. Just imagine that Sisera is sleeping. Jael has given him his milk, tucked him in, and put a little blanket over him. But Sisera is the villain, so Jael quietly grabs a hammer and a tent peg. "Then she drove the tent peg through his temple and into the ground, and so he died. When Barak came looking for Sisera, Jael went out to meet him. She said, 'Come, and I will show you the man you are looking for'" (verses 21–22). Imagine the scene—Barak follows this woman into her home and finds Sisera lying dead with a tent peg in his temple.

Jael knew her value and worth. She also knew the weapons of her warfare and wasn't afraid of a mess. Driving a tent peg into someone's skull is hard and bloody work. She was gangster. She took that tent peg and that hammer and nailed him to the ground.

Jael used what she had. The women were the tent builders. The tents were strong, heavy, and big, which means that the women had some strength. Jael wasn't afraid of the tent peg and hammer, because she was accustomed to constructing tents. Sometimes we take for granted the ordinary things in life like Jael's tent peg, not believing that the supernatural can come forth from the mundane. But God can breathe on the ordinary and make it supernatural.

Sometimes we think, *You know what, God? I need victory over this situation,* but we ignore the everyday items that we possess, like the Bible, the Holy Spirit, or being planted in God's house. Jael used a tent peg and a hammer to help bring forth the victory. What's in your hand? So many people in this world don't have access to Bibles, but we have abundant access to God's Word. We have access to a healthy group of women who we can lean on.

After Jael hammered the tent peg, she could have thought, *What did I do? Oh my goodness. This is so messy. Let me clean it up.* But she wasn't afraid of the mess, because she knew that life is a hot mess at times. She didn't say, "Let me go get someone else for the job." She knew the assignment was hers. And she stepped right into it. Then she walked out to meet Barak. She likely didn't even clean up the blood in her tent. She said, "Come in. Look what I did."

We have to be gangster and hardcore when facing the obstacles before us. We have to see our prayers and our words as weapons until the victory comes. Obviously, this will play out differently for us today. But when the Enemy tries to come into our thoughts, into our homes, or toward what we consider sacred, praying and reading God's Word is our weapon.

Second Corinthians 10:3–5 says, "We are human, but we don't wage war as humans do. We use God's mighty weapons, not worldly weapons, to knock down the strongholds of human reasoning and to destroy false arguments. We destroy every proud obstacle that keeps people from knowing God. We capture their rebellious thoughts and teach them to obey Christ."

Sometimes we get frustrated when things don't turn out the way we want or when life gets messy, but God can do the miraculous in the mess. If your life is messy right now, it's a setup for the miraculous. If your marriage is messy right now, it's a setup for the miraculous. If your thought life is messy right now, it's a setup for the miraculous. God can bring victory in a moment by His presence. Victory isn't something we have to work up in our own strength. We surrender to Him and He brings it.

> *God can do the miraculous in the mess.*

Think about the areas where you need God's victory. How can you believe in victory before it comes just like Deborah did before this battle?

I've walked through some dark situations with loved ones, but declaring truth became a helpful victory practice. I said over and over, "God, I declare victory over this situation." I just kept saying, "I thank You that You're going to make a way. I thank You that You're going to make a way where there seems to be no way." God can do the same for you. A practical way to walk this out is to grab your Bible or phone and look up scriptures on victory. Then insert your name in the verses, and pray them over your situation.

Then, after you cross over to victory, you can help other women cross over to the same.

When our thoughts fixate on our fears of losing the battle, we can draw them back in line through meditating on and praying Scripture. Exodus 15:2 is what I'm declaring over you right now: "The LORD is my strength and my song; he has given me victory. This is my God, and I will praise him—my father's God, and I will exalt him!"

In Romans 8:35, Paul asked, "Can anything ever separate us from Christ's love? Does it mean he no longer loves us if we have trouble or calamity, or are persecuted, or hungry, or destitute, or in danger, or threatened with death?" Verse 37 says, "No," and I love that Paul was so emphatic: "No, despite all these things, overwhelming victory is ours through Christ, who loved us."

Despite all things, overwhelming victory is yours:

Overwhelming victory in your family.
Overwhelming victory in your finances.
Overwhelming victory in your school.
Overwhelming victory in your mind.
Overwhelming victory in your city.
Overwhelming victory is yours through Christ,
    who loves you.

You aren't defeated or inadequate. See yourself as strong, bold, and courageous. One of my favorite scriptures is Philippians 4:13: "I can do everything through Christ, who gives me strength." Our confidence in the battles we face isn't self-talk or hype; it's power, grace, and strength that comes from Christ.

Let's Pray ————————————————————

Jesus, I declare Your victory. I declare Your victory over every battle I'm facing. In faith, I declare victory even before I see victory. Living God, I thank You that Your work is the work of deliverance, breakthrough, and healing. Help me see the work that You are already doing and partner with You in it. Let a value revolution rise up in my heart to deepen my trust in You so I will live more freely into the identity You've given me. May this same value revolution rise up in the hearts of all Your daughters today so we will change our cities and this world for Your glory! Your kingdom come. Amen.

7

GIVE ME ALSO

Before I gave my life to Christ, I didn't understand my value or worth. I didn't know that I was royal and had an inheritance. I settled and made dating decisions that showed I didn't see myself the way Jesus saw me.

Once I started going to church, learning what Jesus said about me, and seeing godly, loving relationships around me, the lies I had believed about my worth and what I deserved fell away little by little. I started to see myself the way Jesus saw me. I started to realize that I was settling and putting up with unacceptable behavior from guys. I even stopped dating for a season and learned to be content with just me and Jesus. He literally rewrote what I was looking for in a future husband and taught me to fall in love with Him and see Him as my first love. Then when I started to date again, I had standards, I had healthy accountability, and I knew my confidence and worth were defined not by my relationship but by Him.

We are God's daughters. We have an inheritance. We have a birthright.

Paul wrote in Galatians 4:7, "Now you are no longer a slave but God's own child." So guess what? It's time to stop acting like a slave. You're an heir. Sometimes we have to remind one another of that.

It can seem easier to go back to living in bondage to our old ways of thinking. But Christ came so that we could live in freedom as part of our inheritance, and who the Son sets free is free indeed.[1] I love this truth.

An inheritance is a birthright, a portion, and a heritage. As God's royal daughter, you have an inheritance in Christ. In the Bible, the birthright was usually given to the oldest son. The one who received it was honored with a double share of his father's inheritance.[2] The birthright also included certain rights and privileges, as well as responsibilities. Since we are believers in Christ, we are given privileges because we share in Christ's inheritance. As adopted daughters of God, we get to be treated as firstborns and heirs.

Here's an example from the Bible where the older son sold his birthright to his younger brother.[3] Let me introduce you to two parents, Isaac and Rebekah, who had twin sons, Jacob and Esau. Isaac loved Esau, and Rebekah loved Jacob. Scripture tells us, "One day when Jacob was cooking some stew, Esau arrived home from the wilderness exhausted and hungry" (Genesis 25:29).

We all do crazy stuff when we're exhausted and hungry. I get hangry, so I always have snacks in my purse. I started snacking eighteen years ago when I was pregnant with Parker, and I just haven't stopped. I might be eating a protein bar or nuts, because I carry a picnic in my purse.

Esau asked Jacob to give him some of the stew he was cooking. Jacob saw an opportunity and told him that he would give him some stew if he sold his birthright. So Esau did. And that's how we see that Esau didn't understand his birthright, because if he had, he wouldn't have sold it for some stew.

Sometimes we don't understand our birthright as God's daughters. We don't understand that we have a purpose and an inheritance. So we trade our Christ-given inheritance for a metaphorical bowl of stew. Esau was the firstborn, so a double portion of the inheritance was coming to him. As heiresses to Christ's inheritance, we have access to every single resource from God our Father's estate. It's so important that we grasp the extent of our inheritance, because once we do, we walk with a different confidence. We don't sell ourselves short for a bowl of soup. Let me ask you, What's your bowl of soup? What are you settling for in your life?

Esau was tired and hungry when he came back from the wilderness. When we're tired and hungry, our guard is down. We settle for what's not best, and we make decisions based on feeling like God has forgotten about us or He's not answering our prayers. Esau didn't value the inheritance that his father was preparing to give him. If he had known what was waiting for him, if he had truly valued his inheritance, he would have said, "You can keep that soup." We need to value our inheritance as God's daughters. When temptation comes our way or when we're discouraged, we think, *I'm just going to camp out in this mediocre relationship. I'm going to camp out in these negative thought patterns. I'm not going to believe God for the purposes and plans that He has for my life.* But you know what? Girl—you're just tired. Put the soup down.

We don't want to give up anything too freely, because our lives, our value, our worth, our purpose, and our future were bought with a price. Christ gave His life to make it possible for us to be heirs. Every single attribute of heaven belongs to us. We have a double portion of inheritance waiting for us if we would just believe it, walk into it, and receive it. I think some of us cling to old mindsets because of our familial background. Some of us have even been taught to limit or devalue ourselves. But God says, "I have more for you." You have an inheritance coming. Wait. You may be hungry now, and you may be tired, but wait.

There's another story involving Esau, Jacob, their parents, and an inheritance.[4] Rebekah, their mother, was once barren, so she and Isaac would cry out to God to become pregnant, believing Him for a miracle. Finally, she was blessed with their twin boys, Jacob and Esau. Her dream of being a mother was fulfilled. You would think that the story goes on to recount how Rebekah served her family and the kingdom of God faithfully because her dream came true, but that wasn't the case. Sometimes, in our desperation, we cry out to God to intervene, and He does, but then we just act foolish. We've all been there, myself included. Well, our girl Rebekah didn't understand her power and influence as a royal daughter.

Genesis 27 tells how Rebekah's husband, Isaac, was getting ready to pass away. His eyes had become dim and he could barely see. Isaac was planning on blessing Esau before he died. But Rebekah overheard their conversation and manipulated Isaac into giving the second son the firstborn's blessing. Many women and men are guilty of this. I'm just going to be real. Sometimes we manipulate a situation because we're hungry, we're tired, we're tired of waiting, or we think God has forgotten us. We then play the puppeteer. We maneuver people and situations into our desired positions so that we can determine the outcome, because we don't trust God.

This is what happened with Rebekah. God was faithful to her. She cried out to Him and said, "Please give me a child!" God then blessed her with twins, but she still decided to not trust Him anymore and instead manipulated the situation to get what she wanted. She convinced her son Jacob to dress up like Esau so that he could receive Isaac's blessing. Rebekah had to take some skin from a goat and tie it to her son's arms and neck, which means she had probably been thinking of this plan for a while. She knew her husband was getting old, and her actions were well thought out.

After Jacob got dressed in Esau's clothes and tied on goatskin so he was as hairy as his brother, Rebekah gave him a delicious meal that she had cooked, which included freshly baked bread. Basically, Rebekah said, "Let's make a meal for your dad. He can barely see. We're going to disguise you and cook his favorite meal so you can get the blessing." Jacob gave the meal to his father. And Isaac, sensing that something was up, asked, "Who are you—Esau or Jacob?" (verse 18). Jacob replied with a lie, which was a practice his mother had taught him.

Do you ever cook somebody their "favorite meal" by writing them a message or buying them a present so you can get what you want? That's manipulation. God has a plan for our lives, and we don't have to play puppet master to get it. We don't have to play God. He knows that you want that man, that job, that house. He knows that you want freedom in a certain area of your life. We don't have to play God like Rebekah did.

The antidote for manipulation is surrender.

If Rebekah had surrendered the desires that she had for her kids, she wouldn't have stepped into manipulation. But because she did, her family was divided. Esau got angry with his brother. He wanted to kill him, so Jacob ran away—all because Rebekah manipulated Isaac into blessing her favorite son. Her actions broke Isaac's heart just like we break the Father's heart when we use the gifts that He has given us to bring about our own will. Instead, we can surrender and say, "God, You know that I want x, y, and z. You know that I want that job. You know that I want to dream again. You know that I'm believing You for healing and for restoration. I trust You. I trust that as I fall back, You are going to catch me. I want to fix my situation, because that's my comfort zone, but I know that You fixed it on the cross. So I don't want to manipulate anymore. I'm going to surrender it to Your will."

If we can grab hold of this message, we can change our cities.

If we can grab hold of this message, we can change our cities. Do you know how many junior high girls need to hear that they are royalty with an inheritance? Do you know how many college girls are starving themselves trying to fit into a certain size because they don't get this truth? If we can understand that we possess an inheritance, we can literally start a value revolution in your city, my city, and beyond. If we start being women who walk in our inheritance, men will treat us correctly. They won't try stupid stuff, because they'll realize that we are God's daughters and His heirs. That's what I love about so many of the men at my home church, Shoreline City. They come early, they stay late, and they serve with humility everywhere in the house because we're raising up a generation of women and men who understand that women are royal daughters. We can walk taller and stand with confidence because Jesus paid the debt of sin for us. We're not limiting ourselves. We have potential. We have purpose. We have value. There's no need to settle.

God offers us more than what we settle for. He's a "more than" God. But we give up sometimes. We don't believe that we are heiresses to God's fortune. So we just run in place, not making progress in our lives. The Enemy wants us to settle and run in place, locked out of the promises of God.

As I've shared previously, I settled for the wrong guys in college. My only prerequisites for a guy were that he be handsome and a Christian. My heart was broken so many times because I kept running in circles by dating the wrong guys. But if I had known that the inheritance of my husband, Earl McClellan, was waiting, I wouldn't have settled.

Because of Christ, we have blessings waiting for us if we don't grow faint or weary. If we will just say, "God, I'm going to stick this out. I'm going to trust You on the hard and good days. I'm going to trust in the power of the blood that Jesus shed on the cross. I'm not going to settle. I'm going to wait until You provide every single thing that I need."

So I want to tell you that God has a blessing for your dreams. He has a blessing for your career. He has a blessing for your family, for your future, and for your relationships. He has prepared an inheritance for you.[5] You just have to step into it and receive it. Thank God I didn't camp in bad relationships. If I had, I would've still been dating this guy named Tony. Oneka and Tony. That combination doesn't even sound right, because it's supposed to be Oneka and Earl. I'm so glad that I said, "God, You have a plan and purpose for me. I'm surrendering my singleness to You. I'm going to stop dating all these boys, and I'm going to trust You." God will provide the right school and the right job for you. He will heal you. He will give you visions and fulfill your dreams. Wait for your inheritance, because it's coming. Once you receive it, you can wake up the other women in your community that are asleep to the plans and purposes of God and say, "He gave me an inheritance, and He'll do the same for you." Or say, "Let's wait for our inheritance together and encourage one another in the wait." We're a sisterhood and we're better together. We value one another. We speak life into one another.

> *God has an inheritance*
> *for you.*

While Earl was on a mission trip, God told him that I was for him. We had the same group of friends in college, and I had a crush on him. Everyone was telling him that he needed to go for me, but he was focusing on basketball, school, and Jesus and didn't want to be distracted by any relationship. Earl then went on this mission trip. He was in India, crying out to God on the country's behalf, but while he was praying, a picture of me kept coming into his mind. At first, he thought Satan had planted the image because he was on a mission trip, so he rebuked the thought. Then he got a clue and realized, *Oh, wait. This is God, and He's telling me I'm supposed to pursue this girl.*

While he was in India, he also went to take a shower in the first stall that he saw, and there sat a bucket of freezing cold water. He poured ladles of it on himself, trying to take some kind of shower. About ten minutes later, a friend of his walked by with steam coming off his body, claiming to have had the best shower. Earl said, "Wait a second—you don't look like you used that bucket with the cold water."

His friend Teddy said, "Just two stalls down, there's a shower with a showerhead and hot water."

What is just two stalls down from you? Some of us have a small mindset and believe that God's favor and blessings will fit in a ladle that we'll need to dump on ourselves when, only two stalls down, our inheritance is waiting for us. Two stalls down, our blessing is coming. Two stalls down, our miracle is coming. Let's stop settling for pouring cold water on ourselves.

God is a God who gives us more than enough. His blessings are endless and overflowing. He doesn't set limitations on us. He doesn't box us in. He sees endless possibilities in and for us. That's the God we serve. We've pitched a tent in the world, accepting its way of defining our identity and treating other women. Meanwhile, He's waiting for His royal daughters to receive our inheritance. So I want you to start seeing endless possibilities for your life and the women around you.

If we start a value revolution, if we stop settling, if we walk in our inheritance, if we change the way the world sees women and the way women see one another, just think about how many people will come to know Christ. Think about how many women's walls of insecurity and self-protection will come down when they meet another woman who is speaking life to them and not competing with them or judging them. You have what it takes to start a value revolution, because God has brought you to this moment for such a time as this. He's entrusting you with this word. We're going to be carriers of Christ's revolution for women, and it will spread all throughout our cities and beyond.

I dare you to speak life to someone you don't know. Be ready for God to move miraculously in that woman's life and in your life by your speaking words of value to her. Do you have difficult people in your family? I know I do. Write them letters that speak life to them. Speak life in the midst of all the crazy.

One particular woman in Joshua 15:16–19 really grasped the importance of her inheritance and was confident in her identity. A man named Caleb promised his daughter to the man who would attack and capture a city he had been assigned in the promised land. Well, a man named Othniel captured the city, so Caleb gave him his daughter to marry and gave the couple land. But this woman knew her father and asked him for something more. Do you know your Father in heaven like this woman knew her father, Caleb? Do you know that you can ask Him for anything? The daughter rode to meet her father and said, "Do me a special favor. Since you have given me land in the Negev, give me also springs of water" (verse 19, NIV). And Caleb gave her what she asked for.

Caleb's daughter didn't think small or limit her father's capabilities. She said, "Give me also."

God is looking for royal daughters who will say, "Give me also. I'm not going to settle for only what's in front of me."

We serve a God who is more than enough.

Give me also breakthrough in my family.

Give me also healing in my body.

Give me also salvation for my entire family.

Give me also favor in my job.

Give me also strength to wake up tomorrow and crush it.

Give me also peace in my mind when negative thoughts come.

We're not eating the stew anymore. We're not camping out in mediocrity anymore. We're going to walk into the promises of God because we serve a God who has given us an inheritance.

Of course, we don't have a magic wand to wave, and we don't make demands of God, but this heart posture reminds us to not settle and to know that He wants what is best for us. Just like my little girl isn't afraid to ask her daddy for anything—and I do mean anything—we shouldn't be afraid to ask our heavenly Father for our hearts' desires. Matthew 6:27–30 says, "Can all your worries add a single moment to your life? And why worry about your clothing? Look at the lilies of the field and how they grow. They don't work or make their clothing, yet Solomon in all his glory was not dressed as beautifully as they are. And if God cares so wonderfully for wildflowers that are here today and thrown into the fire tomorrow, he will certainly care for you."

What's your "give me also" for your family? What's your "give me also" for your thoughts, your job, your school, your finances, and your city? God has decreed that He is moving in your neighborhood. He is moving in your heart. I'm praying that this stirs your faith. I'm believing that if we're all praying for one another's family, for breakthroughs, for our communities, then we will break the limits we've placed on ourselves. What do you think will happen? A value revolution. Chains will break. The lost will come home. The broken will be healed. I'm believing that you will stop limiting God and you will remember that you have an inheritance as His royal daughter. Let's step into what God has for us, our families, our cities, and this world. We are the carriers of His vision, His Spirit, and His life.

To understand our value and our inheritance, we must surrender everything to Jesus. So, in this moment, we're surrendering every single thing, every single plan, and every single dream to Christ. With surrendered hearts, let's ask and believe God for miracles. We surrender all to You, Jesus. We surrender.

Let's Pray

Dear Jesus, thank You that You have given me a spirit not of fear but of power, love, and a sound mind. Help me not sell myself short. I will no longer settle. I will look to You for my career, school, and relationship dreams.
I trust You to decide what is best for me. I will not let this world pressure me into lowering my value and worth.
I thank You that You have my best interests in mind, and I commit to putting my hope and trust in You.

8

EQUIPPED TO FIGHT

When I was preparing this chapter, I was thinking about different fights in this world and then I remembered when I was in elementary school and I got into a fight. The class was bullied by a girl named Jean who had a bowl haircut. She picked on everyone; she owned the playground as the self-appointed boss. She also was taller than all of us and used her height and strength to lord it over us. She was one of those kids that no one crossed. She just brought fear with her everywhere she went. Finally, one day I decided to do something. With my cute little press and curl, which is when your hair is really curly and tight, I said to myself, *Today Jean is about to meet her match.*

I told Jean, "It's not fair that you're bullying everybody." And then I don't know what came over me, but I hit her. For a moment, I felt proud of myself, but before I could blink, she popped me back so hard I literally saw stars. But I got back up.

Sometimes in life, we get knocked down by marriage problems, knocked down by stress in school, and knocked down by our dreams being delayed. But in this moment, God's saying, "Girl, I've crowned you to fight."

Which of us really knows how to fight for what we believe in? Which of us knows how to fight in prayer and cry out to God for breakthroughs? If you haven't found your fight, if you've lost your fight, or if you need to be reminded to fight, I'm betting that by the time you finish this chapter, you'll be ready, 'cause, baby, you're worth it.

Esther 4:14 says, "Perhaps you have come to your royal position for such a time as this" (CSB). I was thinking about the state of our nation and world, and it's easy to just get discouraged with the news and all the negativity we see on social media. But guess what? We've been called to fight. We've been crowned for such a time as this. This very moment, God isn't surprised by the state of the world. We are part of the solution. We are part of the change that we want to see on this earth. We are part of the breakthrough. We weren't alive a hundred years ago; we are alive now. God has called us to make a difference in our time. We don't want to complain about the world we live in, and we don't want to complain about the future. We want to fight for it. That fight happens in prayer, and that fight happens when we know that we've been crowned for it.

Sometimes you don't choose the fight. The fight chooses you.

God wants you to hold your position. I don't know what you're fighting in your mind, I don't know what you're fighting from your past, but God wants to fight with you. So keep persevering so that you're not completely knocked out. He wants you to bounce back. We've been crowned for the fight. Some of us were born into a fight. Some of us have to face fights that we didn't plan or want. But remember, "you have come to your royal position for such a time as this."

We've been crowned for the fight.

I think about a beautiful mom in our church. She fights every single day for her little girl. She goes to more doctors' appointments than she can count and has visited the ER more than she ever would desire. But despite all this, she knows that she is crowned for the fight. Every single time she opens her mouth, she's speaking praise, she's speaking blessing, and she's speaking faith. She didn't choose this fight for her little girl, but she has embraced the fight and is standing her ground. I'm praying and fighting with her.

I think about another one of my friends, Lauren Kuehn. Several years ago, she was diagnosed with cancer. She fought that battle with every single ounce of energy within her. I was fighting for her and fighting with her. If you had spent two seconds around her, you wouldn't have felt sorry for her. Your faith would've been encouraged, and you would've been energized, because she knew she was crowned for the fight. Although her story didn't end the way I had believed and prayed for, I'm forever marked by her fighting spirit. She didn't choose that fight. She didn't want cancer to be her story, but she dusted her gloves off and said, "Bring it on, devil. What do you have for me now?"

One day during her journey with cancer, a few of us went to lunch for her birthday, and this is what she said: "I don't want any presents. I just want to speak life and God's Word into our hearts." So we sat at the table, and she spoke life into each one of us. She spoke to our futures; she spoke to our potential; she spoke to the call of God on our lives. She was a mom of four who was engaged in her own fight, yet she was still calling out the fight in all of us. No matter what battle you're facing, God knows what it is, and He wants to wake up the fight in you and inspire you to be all that He's called you to be.

First Corinthians 15:57 says, "Thank God! He gives us victory over sin and death through our Lord Jesus Christ." When Christ died on the cross for us, His fight guaranteed our victory. Those old thought patterns you're fighting, He took them to the cross and guaranteed your victory. This is such good news.

Right before Jesus went to the cross, He cried out to God in prayer. He said to His disciples, "I'm going to go just a stone's throw away to pray. Y'all pray with me." The Bible says in Luke 22:44 that He was in such great anguish that His sweat was like drops of blood. He was in a fight for the world, and the fight was agonizing. Anguish isn't pretty, pain isn't pretty, but He took on all the agony so we would know that the victory is ours. We just have to step into the victory that Christ has already won.

Psalm 144:1 says, "Praise the LORD, who is my rock." Who needs Him to be their rock today? The verse continues, "He trains my hands for war and gives my fingers skill for battle." God is not afraid of battle, and He's not afraid of war. The thing is, we don't have to fight by ourselves. He's going to anoint us and strengthen us to be able to fight every battle that comes our way.

In the early stages of my friend Lauren's battle with cancer, we were texting about fight songs. Worship is our fight song. Worship is how we acquire victory. Worship is how we endure the battle. Worship is where we realize breakthrough. So, right after she was diagnosed, Lauren and I were texting, and we both just started singing, "I will live and not die and tell of the works of God."[1] We started declaring God's presence over her. We started declaring healing over her. Worship was our weapon. We worshipped over that diagnosis all the way until her last day.

Our reward is heaven, our home. As much as we enjoy life here on earth, the Bible says it's but a vapor.[2] So even though my best friend, Lauren, wasn't healed on earth and even though I miss her every single day, I find rest knowing that she is no longer suffering. I find peace knowing that she is probably painting, dancing, and singing at the feet of Jesus. No more medicine, no more pain—pure, unending joy. What eternal victory.

No matter what battle you're facing, remember you're equipped with powerful weapons. I talked in chapter 5 about the power of worship while we're in battle. But worship isn't our only weapon. I've talked about another weapon all throughout this book. That weapon is God's Word, our Bibles. When I'm in a battle and even when I'm not, you will find me blasting worship music, reading my Bible, and praying Scripture over my situation. I also listen to powerful and encouraging sermons to fill me up. Another practical thing I do is leave other people voice memos and text messages speaking life over them. What I've found is that watering others helps me get my mind off myself and lifts my head above the clouds.

My pastor, Laura Koke, is a fighter, y'all. She's one of the toughest, baddest women I know. She fights on her knees in prayer. She lives in a constant state of surrender. After her teenage son passed away, she had every excuse to stop fighting. In grief, she wisely took time to rest and heal. But she now fights for those who have lost loved ones. She didn't and doesn't just stop with her own needs. She has mentored and fought for a trail of women around the world that follow her example as she teaches them how to fight, how to stand tall, how to remain faithful, and how to keep Jesus at the center. There were so many days when I felt like giving up after starting to pastor my own church with my husband. But Pastor Laura rejoiced with me in the small victories and prayed over me with faith and conviction in every discouragement. She was mentoring me when the first five people joined our church and is still mentoring me now that thousands around the world are part of our church. She still rejoices with me, still cries with me, and still prays with me through the highs and the lows of building our church.

Jesus fought for us, so we need to fight for the girls in our world. God doesn't hold back. He doesn't just sit back and let life slap us up and down; He teaches our hands to fight the battle. We've got to imagine a new picture of Jesus. Sometimes we think that He's just chilling with a blankie when really He's straight gangster and knows how to battle.

Listen to David's words in Psalm 18:29: "In your strength I can crush an army; with my God I can scale any wall." David knew God because he met with God so many times. God wants you to call Him your personal God.

David went on, "He trains my hands for battle; he strengthens my arm to draw a bronze bow" (verse 34). Too many times we try to tackle problems in our own strength. We try to tackle trouble at work in our own strength. We try to raise kids in our own strength. But God says, "Let Me teach you how to war. Let Me train you."

David's words are bold: "I chased my enemies and caught them; I did not stop until they were conquered. . . . You have armed me with strength for the battle; you have subdued my enemies under my feet. You placed my foot on their necks" (verses 37, 39–40). Wow. Those are fighting words.

Some of us need to wake up that grit within us. We need to stop being passive, stop being a victim of the Enemy's schemes, stop letting him invade our minds, and stop letting him rob our joy. Take your foot, and put it on the Enemy's neck in the name of Jesus, because evil is already defeated.

"He is the God who pays back those who harm me" (verse 47). This is a word of freedom because it tells us we don't have to spend our lives hunting down the people who have harmed us. God is going to pay back those enemies. He's got your back. He knows who hurt you, He knows who wronged you, and He knows what fights you were dragged into that you didn't choose. But again, He is the God who pays back.

In the boxing movie *Rocky*, there are two main characters, Rocky and Mickey.[3] At different times in our lives, we're either Rocky, throwing punches in the fight, or we're Mickey, aiding someone in their fight. When we're in the fight, we need the Mickeys in our sisterhood to say, "You're going to get through this. I see a jab coming your way, girl, so break up with him. I see a jab. I see a one-two punch to your right. So break up." The Mickeys in our lives say, "I see you picking up those old habits again." They confront sin and faulty mindsets and bad habits. We need the Mickeys.

When we're in the fight, we need to remember that we're not alone and that God has strengthened us. But once we get our victory, once we get that heavyweight title, we don't need to just put it up on our mantel. At times, we have to assume the role of Mickey too.

We need to take our victory, find other women who need a Mickey, and tell them that they can get victory too. We need to cheer them on and remind them what's possible:

> I got that promotion I thought would never come my way,
> so you can too.
> I survived freshman year, so you can too.
> I got through financial struggles, so you can too.
> I got through the sleepless newborn season, so you can too.
> I got through being a single mom, so you can too.

My friend Holly went through a season of feeling alone and having no friends. She now has more friends than she can count on one hand. Instead of staying stuck, she became the kind of friend she wanted for herself. She pursued people, and now all these years later, her life is full of beautiful friendships and she gets to help other girls find friends.

I think about Ronda Rousey, a phenomenal professional wrestler and MMA fighter. Rousey's mom is also a fighter. Every day, she would wake up her daughter and practice this wrestling move called an arm bar with her so that the move was ingrained in her fighting style.[4] The arm bar became her signature move. What we see from this mother-daughter duo is that we fight for ourselves and the next generation. We're not going to raise a passive generation of women. We're going to teach the next generation to fight for what they believe in, to fight God's way, and to call out their dreams. Unfortunately, Rousey lost her last fight. One news reporter claimed that Rousey's room was quiet and somber before she walked to the ring for her last UFC fight.[5] I wondered if maybe, in that moment, she had lost her fight song. No anthem was playing in her room, so when she got into the ring, she got knocked out.

We need a fight song. We can't just be quiet, still, and passive and wait as opportunities pass by. We've got to shout out the anthems of God. We've got to shout out our fight song and declare, "Victory is mine in the name of Jesus. I'm going to make it. It seems like I'm not right now. I feel defeated in this moment, but through Christ I can do all things." We need to reclaim our fight song. We need to remember that we've been crowned to fight.

As royal daughters, we haven't been crowned to sit in the palace; we've been crowned to fight in the field. Second Chronicles 20:15 says, "This is what the LORD says: 'Do not be afraid! Don't be discouraged by this mighty army, for the battle is not yours, but God's.'" Your family is not yours, but God's. Your kids are not yours, but God's.

He wants to wake up the fighter in us. This world we live in requires a supernatural strength and a fighting spirit that won't back down. He gives us the will, desire, and ability to get in the ring and stay in the ring. He gives us the power to defeat our opponent. If we were left to our own strength, we would be only fighting the wind and running in circles. Can I get an amen?

So remember, the fight that you're facing is not yours alone, but God's. Whatever it is that you can't take one more day of is not yours, but God's. God is saying, "Sweetheart, let Me carry that for you. Sweetheart, let Me fight this one for you. Sweetheart, let Me remind you that I will be your anthem and your strong tower." You've been crowned to fight, not to sit back.

One Hebrew word for "crown" is *atarah* and comes from a verb that means "to encircle (for attack or protection)."[6] Our position as royal daughters means we come alongside and encircle others; we look out for one another and fight beside one another. It's a way of being in relationship that says, "I got your back. I'm not going to stand against you; I'm going to stand up for you." It's a posture, not a pose.

Don't give up. You're not alone. I believe by the Spirit of God that you're going to get your fight back, that you're going to get your sight back, that you're going to get hope, and that you're going to get freedom and peace.

Don't lose heart. You have a whole army of women surrounding you and cheering you on.

This world is waiting and ready. We've got to fight for one another, not bully or judge one another. I want to fight for my fellow women from now until eternity because we don't have time for petty stuff. So I'm calling you to rise up and fight for the women on your right and your left.

Let's Pray ———————————————

Father, I'd like to thank You that we're starting a value revolution in Your daughters around the world. I thank You that You have equipped us to fight the battles we're facing with confidence that the victory is already won. We're going to fight for one another because You fight for us. I thank You that greater days are ahead. I thank You that we don't have to do this alone. With Jesus on our side, we move ahead. Bless every person reading this, and strengthen us in Jesus's name. Amen.

9

GIFTED TO LEAD

I have a hunch that most of us lead far more often than we think we do. I think about the times you and I didn't even realize we were leading, like when you heard girls gossiping and you stood up for the person being gossiped about. Or when you led a committee at your child's school or a Bible study with friends in your dorm, or when you were a role model on a sports teams or at a company, and everything in between.

You were made to lead. You were made to make things better.

You were made to
make things better.

I love leading most days. In a previous chapter, I talked about leading our church during 2020. That was a season when leading was extremely stressful and overwhelming, and at times, it almost felt impossible. As my husband and I led together, it seemed as though no matter how much we gave, it still was never enough.

No one said leading is easy. But leading is necessary. I've heard it said that leaders go first. And in going first, we pioneer and we also partner with the people God has placed around us. There is no way my husband and I could lead our church without the help of Jesus, our staff, and our volunteers.

Leadership is pioneering and partnering, and it's also serving. Jesus showed us the ultimate example when He washed the feet of His disciples.[1] He took a towel from around His waist and took on the posture of a servant. That is a position not of lording it over people but of confident humility.

Our world is desperate for you as God's daughter to take your heaven-breathed authority and stand firm in every season.

Leadership is also lonely at times. Matthew 26:37–45 says that Jesus asked His disciples to pray with Him but they all fell asleep. I'm sure at that moment He felt alone and disappointed. I've had moments in my leadership when I've felt alone, disappointed, and misunderstood. But I've learned that God uses it all to refine me and keep my gaze on Him. I'm not leading to get a platform, more followers, a trophy, or a pat on the back. I'm leading because He called me to, and the same is true for you. Just like Esther, we are called to lead for such a time as this.

Second Kings 2 tells us about the prophet Elijah and his mentee, Elisha, journeying together. When they started out, they were going from Gilgal to Bethel. From there, they traveled to Jericho, then to the Jordan River. Elijah knew his time was almost finished on earth, and all throughout their long journey together, he basically gave Elisha multiple chances to leave him. But Elisha said to Elijah, "As surely as the LORD lives and you yourself live, I will never leave you" (verses 2, 4, 6). Elisha wanted Elijah's mantle and anointing.

Elijah took his cloak—a symbol of God's presence and authority—and struck the water of the Jordan River. The river miraculously divided, and the two men crossed on dry land. Then Elijah said to his student, "Tell me what I can do for you before I am taken away" (verse 9).

Elisha replied, "Please let me inherit a double share of your spirit and become your successor" (verse 9).

"You have asked a difficult thing," Elijah said, and he instructed Elisha to keep his eyes on him and on God's presence (verse 10). Soon after, Elijah went up in a whirlwind to heaven. Elisha watched his mentor go, then picked up his cloak.

In our nation and in our world, there's a cloak; there's a mantle; there's an anointing that has fallen. As God's daughters, it's time for us to pick up the mantle so that we can receive our double portion by the Spirit of the Lord.

Elisha went back to the Jordan River and remembered what his leader had done there. So "he struck the water with Elijah's cloak and cried out, 'Where is the LORD, the God of Elijah?' " Then the river divided and Elisha went across (verse 14). How powerful is that?

He picked up where his leader left off.

I think about all the women who have gone before us. It's time for us to pick up where they left off.

When it comes to leadership, most of us fall into two categories.

First, there is the "failure to launch" leader. Do you know the movie *Failure to Launch*?[2] The one with Matthew McConaughey? McConaughey plays the main character, who refuses to move out of his parents' house. He just stays there, playing video games and hanging out with friends. He never wants to step out and be all he's called to be. It's time for some of us to ask ourselves what's holding us back. We have no excuse to not be all God has called us to be.

Others of us have recognized that we're leaders, and we've launched into leadership like an astronaut in a space shuttle. But here's the problem: We're the only passenger. We're headed to the top, doing our thing—moving, grooving, slaying, taking land, just going for it. But we haven't brought any women with us to mentor on the journey. There's no passing of the baton. God is challenging me and challenging you to bring other women along with us. No matter where you are in life, look around for other God-honoring women and encourage them to keep walking with integrity.

Bringing others along can look as simple as living with integrity. For example, I make a point to avoid gossip. When I come across it in conversation, I try to find a gentle way to end that train of talk. I'll say something like, "We're not going to tear her down with gossip. We don't know her story or her situation." This is leading in the moment, and those around us might be encouraged to follow along as we try to live with integrity. Whether you're in high school or college, on the bottom rung at your corporation or in the C-suite, you can lead in this way. Gossip happens in the workplace and among stay-at-home moms, but we can lead by not gossiping and by challenging others to do the same. We can also lead by not filling in the wrong blank when we don't understand something. When someone doesn't call us back, we can lead in that moment by giving the benefit of the doubt to that person.

Bringing others along as we lead can look a lot of ways. A woman who is a boss in real estate pours into her community by serving at church and mentoring other people on their journey. My friend Rachel, the worship leader at my church, just pours out her life while being a fantastic mother. From the time her son, Harrison, was just six weeks old, she was breastfeeding in between leading worship and still leading like a boss by pastoring, loving people, and singing. She's launching into God's call on her own life, but she's also raising up an army of younger worship leaders to do the same. Another friend, Summer Graham, who is a major event planner, just had a baby and still shows up to serve at my church every week. She leads our serving teams with strength and grace.

The key is that we have to teach other women to walk in their calling and equip them along the way. You can be rocking and rolling, doing your own thing, but teach somebody else what you're doing so they can succeed as well. Then when it's time to pass your baton like Elijah, you have an Elisha who is ready to take up your mantle so the mission doesn't end with you.

Ephesians 4:1–3 says, "In light of all this, here's what I want you to do. While I'm locked up here, a prisoner for the Master, I want you to get out there and walk—better yet, run!—on the road God called you to travel. I don't want any of you sitting around on your hands. I don't want anyone strolling off, down some path that goes nowhere. And mark that you do this with humility and discipline—not in fits and starts, but steadily, pouring yourselves out for each other in acts of love" (MSG). Isn't that good?

We need to master a few disciplines to lead effectively.

Lead Your Mind

The first one is to lead your thoughts. God has called you to lead no matter if you're in school, at home, or in the workplace. No matter where your feet touch, you're called to lead. Let's be leaders in our responses and our attitudes. How about that? Let's be leaders in our mindsets.

No one can lead your mind except you.

When we notice we're thinking overly negative thoughts about ourselves or others, we are the only person who can effectively interrupt those thoughts and replace them with the truth of God's Word. When fearful ideas rise in our minds, we can compassionately lead ourselves by slowing our thoughts down, thinking carefully about whether what we fear is real or not and reasonable or not, and then considering what we should do about it.

We have a lot more power to change the way we think than we realize.

Lead for Legacy

We lead because of the legacy of women who have gone before us. Sometimes we just take women's contributions for granted, but there was a day when women couldn't vote and didn't have a voice. There was a time when our opinions didn't matter. There was a time when we were overlooked. There was a time when a woman would have been skipped over for a job in favor of a man. Now, those days are fading and we do have a voice. It's so important that we realize that other women fought for our current rights, and we can't take their effort for granted. We have to use the leverage they gained for God's glory. He's called us to conquer, to take land, and to do amazing things for His kingdom. But we have to know that our current position comes from the strength and the sacrifice of a generation that's gone before us.

We have a great cloud of witnesses of women in heaven saying, "You do it, girl. You get that baby ready and you get to church and you host. You do it, girl. You go back to school and get that degree. You do it, girl. You tell people about Jesus on your campus and invite them to church."

All the women who paved the way for us are cheering us on, along with all the women in the Bible. We have to stand on their shoulders. It's time for us to pick up the cloak and to stand tall and steward the calling of God well. Someone had to make a way for us. Let's go first to make a way for those behind us. Let's be the ones who are ushering in revival and leading others toward salvation. Invite people to your church. Invite them to come to know

Christ. Have someone over for coffee, tell them your story, and invite them to come to know Jesus. I came to know Jesus because someone just invited me to church and my life was changed.

So many women fought so many battles and sacrificed so much, many giving their lives, so that we could have an inheritance and be daughters of Christ Jesus. Let's keep that momentum going. We don't want to leave the cloak on the floor. We've got to pick it up and carry it by telling other people about God's goodness and faithfulness.

Lead When It's Hard

We have to lead when it's hard and when it's not convenient. When troubles press us on every side, we've still got to lead and step into God's calling on our lives. Pressures weigh on our minds, struggles press on our families, and drama complicates our relationships. Sometimes situations occur that make no sense at all. But listen to what 2 Corinthians 4:8–9 says: "We are pressed on every side by troubles, but we are not crushed. We are perplexed, but not driven to despair. We are hunted down, but never abandoned by God. We get knocked down, but we are not destroyed."

Lead Offstage

Here's another one for you: Lead when you don't get the credit. Leading well isn't about our name in lights. It's all about His glory. Lately, I've been thinking about the favor and blessing of God that He has bestowed on all of us. He's just so good. Some comments on your Instagram posts might tell you how wonderful or beautiful you are. You may have millions of followers. Maybe you have a great talent. But here's some perspective to keep us all humble: People love us, are following us, and see something in us because we're carriers of God's presence. People are attracted to Jesus on the inside of us. I know that I am where I am today, not because I think I'm somebody but because I'm a daughter of God that has chosen to say, "Yes, I will speak up for the girls. Yes, I want to place value on this generation. Yes, I want to get up early and pray when I'm sleepy. Yes, I want to be the woman of God that You've called me to be." But the thing is, when the applause fades and I'm not standing on a platform, I'm called to steward His presence. I'm called to decrease so that He would increase.[3] The same applies to you. No matter how many accolades you get, no matter how many cheers you receive, it's all for His glory.

Leading doesn't look like always being in the spotlight, getting all the credit, likes, or followers. Leading sometimes can look like everyone loving you and you having more followers than you can count, but other times it's a season like Jesus went through when Peter denied even knowing Him. The win of good leadership isn't applause or acceptance from people. The win is obedience to God. That's worth saying again. The win isn't the praise of people; it's giving glory and honor to God. The win isn't about our name; it's about His name. When we seek to push others forward and place value on others, we can find our confidence and definition of success in how He is pleased with us, instead of putting all our hope in the pursuit of being out front. The truth is, leadership is the ability to go first and the humility to be at peace and find joy even when we're last. Matthew 20:16 says,

"Those who are last now will be first then, and those who are first will be last."

Our every action should be to bring Him praise, so let's carry that mission as leaders and steward it well.

Lead with Humility

Last, in humility, we lay our crowns down at the feet of Jesus. Revelation 4:9–11 says, "Every time the Animals gave glory and honor and thanks to the One Seated on the Throne—the age-after-age Living One—the Twenty-four Elders would fall prostrate before the One Seated on the Throne. They worshiped the age-after-age Living One. They threw their crowns at the foot of the Throne, chanting, Worthy, O Master! Yes, our God! Take the glory! the honor! the power!" (MSG).

Can we be women who pray, "Take my family; take my career; take my education—take everything for Your glory because You created it all. My life was created because You wanted it"?

Let's be humble women. Let's not be snobby and unapproachable. Let's walk in the blessings of God with humility. Let's use all the blessings that He bestows on us to help others. Let's lay our crowns and our accolades at the feet of Jesus because He is the one who deserves all glory, all honor, and all praise.

Let's Pray ————————————————————

Dear Jesus, thank You for equipping me to lead and

serve others. Thank You for helping me walk in humility

and strength. Thank You for giving me wisdom and strategy from heaven. Thank You for speaking through me, leading through me, and preparing me for what's ahead. I take off any crowns, and I give You the honor and glory. Please go before me, and remind me that the favor and position I have come from You.

10

CROWNED TO SERVE

We live in a day when so much focus is on building your brand, your own kingdom, your own little world around you. In our culture, if a certain endeavor isn't serving our comfort, our convenience, or our benefit, then it's looked down on. In my humble opinion, in the last few years, many of us realized that in the blink of an eye all that we hold dear can disappear. I think the unexpected outcome of that realization is a mindset of "What's in it for me?"

Now, don't get me wrong. I want you to crush your business, to be successful and at the top in your industry. Whether you're an influencer, entrepreneur, student, or stay-at-home mom, I'm cheering you on to be all that God has called you to be. Don't hold back. But in your pursuit, don't forget the posture of our Savior. He came to lead, but He also came to serve.

When I was praying about this chapter, I struggled at first

because I thought the content might sound cliché. But then God brought me to Mark 10:45: "Even the Son of Man came not to be served but to serve others and to give his life as a ransom for many." This verse says that Jesus set the example of service. He wore a crown of thorns, not just to give humanity value but to serve us. He served us with His life, but He also served us with His death because that act guaranteed eternal life for all who would receive Him. We are crowned to serve, because our Jesus was crowned to serve.

So many women have paved the way for us. So many women in biblical history were hidden figures in aiding the ministry of Jesus. I think of Mary Magdalene, Susanna, Joanna, and the many others who supported Jesus and His disciples out of their own resources.[1] Those women serving in the early days set the foundation for our service today. We're standing on their shoulders.

Women were the major witnesses of Jesus's birth, crucifixion, and His resurrection. When Christians were meeting in houses during the expansion of the early church, women were there. When Christianity was just getting started, did you know that high-class, wealthy women were some of the first to believe and accept Jesus as Savior?[2] They got rowdy about it.

Women started outnumbering men in the early church. The women who were pioneers in the church received a lot of flak for their service because people couldn't understand why they were spending their money on the poor. Their actions might not have made sense, but these women didn't let the fear of being misunderstood hold them back from serving Christ. Even in the early church, women knew that they were crowned to serve. "The women's spiritual zeal exploded into social service," and it was a woman who "founded the first Christian hospital in Europe."[3] Again, women throughout the history of the church have known that they were crowned to serve.

> *Don't let the fear of being*
> *misunderstood hold you back*
> *from serving Christ.*

Some women included in the Bible's pages were just present to support the cause of Christ. They were just there. The writers might not have included them as active characters in the story, but still, they were there. So we have to pick up their mantle and carry their legacy into the next generation. We can't afford to sleep at our posts. We have too many lives to touch. Our nations, our cities, and our communities are looking for women in this millennium who are crowned to serve and are willing to step outside themselves.

In John 10, we're introduced to Lazarus, a really good friend of Jesus. One day when Jesus was out ministering amid political and religious tension, He received word from Lazarus's sisters, Mary and Martha, that Lazarus was really sick. A couple of days passed, and then Jesus said to His disciples, "Let's go back to Judea." The disciples protested because, a few days before, the people in Judea had tried to kill Him.[4] But Jesus said, "Our friend Lazarus has fallen asleep, but now I will go and wake him up." Well, by that time, Lazarus had already died. And miraculously, Jesus raised him from the dead.

Sometimes we don't want to step out of our comfort zones to serve other people because of the inconvenience. But on the other side of our serving, a miracle is waiting. A little while later, Jesus went back to Martha and Mary's to have dinner with them. John emphasized the importance of this meeting: "Jesus arrived in Bethany, the home of Lazarus—the man he had raised from the dead."[5]

I wanted to give you context and texture so that as we go through the story, you can feel and understand the scene. People who were mourning were now celebrating because Lazarus was alive. Imagine losing a loved one, then seeing them come back to life. Imagine Jesus and Lazarus, the healer and the healed, sitting together at the same table. John set the scene for us: "A dinner was prepared in Jesus' honor. Martha served, and Lazarus was among those who ate with him. Then Mary took a twelve-ounce jar of expensive perfume made from essence of nard, and she anointed Jesus' feet with it, wiping his feet with her hair. The house was filled with the fragrance."[6]

I want to pause on that moment for a second. Mary was serving her Savior because she was grateful that her brother was no longer dead. Some of your loved ones have been metaphorically dead, but then God has brought them back to life. You thought that they would never step foot in church after what they've endured, but they're sitting beside you, alive again. So you're crowned to serve because you're grateful. That's what I'm praying for—that our hearts would be filled with such gratitude.

Women might ordinarily have served a rabbi like Jesus, but Mary was also sitting and listening to His teaching and engaging in the conversation. Then, Mary finished dinner. Scripture says, "She anointed His feet, wiping them with her hair. The house was filled with fragrance." As I was studying this passage, I learned that women were careful to cover their hair in Jesus's day. By uncovering hers, Mary was opening herself up to be misunderstood because, in Jewish society at this time, it wasn't proper or respectable to expose your hair in this way.[7] But because Mary was crowned to serve in that moment, she was willing to take that chance. Because she was so grateful, she washed Jesus's feet with her hair. Jesus's feet were dusty because He had been traveling. She washed them anyway. His feet were eventually going to stumble toward the cross, and she washed them in preparation for that journey.

Mary was misunderstood but in a different way. The story continues with Judas Iscariot saying, "That perfume was worth a year's wages. It should have been sold and the money given to the poor."[8] But Judas didn't care for the poor; he was a thief and often helped himself to the disciples' money. Judas was a hater, and tension lay heavy in the room. But Jesus stepped in and said, "Leave her alone. She did this in preparation for my burial. You will always have the poor among you, but you will not always have me" (verses 7–8). Imagine that moment. Mary was just hanging out with Jesus, and her heart was overwhelmed and filled with gratitude for the miracle He had performed for her family. She spent an entire year's wages, which is what that little twelve-ounce jar was worth, and she poured it out on Jesus's feet and poured her heart out in service. I just think this story is so beautiful.

I've been married for a long time now, which is so awesome. I can't even believe it. My heart is filled with such gratitude. I want to pour oil on the feet of Jesus. I want to give Him every single thing I have and serve Him with every fiber of my being because—here's the deal—my parents weren't married. I didn't get to see a godly example of a husband and wife. Bedtime stories weren't read to me every night like Earl and I do for our kids. I'm rewriting history, and I'm so grateful that Jesus set me free and painted a picture of a healthy marriage for me. So I'm honored to serve. I'm honored to serve my husband. Honored to serve in the church. Honored to serve my sisters. Just twenty-five years ago, I was at a club in a cropped top dropping it like it was hot. I know that I don't have it all together, and I know that God isn't finished with me yet, but I'm so grateful. So I want to give Him my all.

It's my prayer that we would be so grateful that we would want to give Him everything and serve our families, our communities, and the local church. I pray that we would want to pour out everything at whatever cost because of that gratitude. When Mary acted out of her gratitude, the Bible says, "The house was filled with the fragrance" (verse 3). If you've ever wondered why the church that you go to is so special, it's because a group of women and men who know that they're crowned to serve lead by laying down their lives. The house is then filled with His fragrance. Or think of an organization you admire like the Red Cross, the Salvation Army, or March of Dimes. Those organizations are made up of people who volunteer, and that generosity of service is a large part of what makes them so special.

John 13 tells us about the final Passover that Jesus celebrated with His disciples. "Jesus knew that his hour had come to leave this world and return to his Father. He had loved his disciples during his ministry on earth, and now he loved them to the very end" by serving them (verse 1). Even though His life was at risk, He was at dinner with His disciples. Anyone could knock on the door at any moment to take His life. But they were having dinner together, and "he got up from the table, took off his robe, wrapped a towel around his waist, and poured water into a basin" (verses 4–5).

I love that our Savior, who we should serve, exemplified how we should serve others. He easily could have said, "I'm about to suffer and die for all of you. Can you all wash My feet and say nice things about Me?" But that's not what He did. He knew that He would soon wear a crown of thorns, but in that moment, He knew that He was crowned to serve.

Think about this: Would so much conflict exist in our families, so much drama take place in our friendships, so much division run amok in our communities, if we knew that we were crowned to serve one another well? "Each of you should use whatever gift you have received to serve others, as faithful stewards of God's grace in its various forms" (1 Peter 4:10, NIV).

How beautiful would the transformation be if we all modeled servant behavior in our marriages? If we knew we were crowned to serve those in our workplaces, would we have peace? If we knew we were crowned to serve those at church, would it feel more like home? Jesus knew that He was crowned to serve, and He knew that His service was preparing Him for death. When we serve like Jesus served, it prepares us to die to self. Serving others without personal gain will kill selfishness.

Jesus got vulnerable with His disciples, stripped off His outer garments, and was just raw and real with them. Mary had washed Jesus's feet, and then He in turn washed the disciples' feet. "After washing their feet, he put on his robe again and sat down and asked, 'Do you understand what I was doing? You call me "Teacher" and "Lord," and you are right, because that's what I am. And since I, your Lord and Teacher, have washed your feet, you ought to wash each other's feet.' "[9] Whatever backgrounds we have, whatever situations we are in, we are crowned to serve and to wash the feet of our sisters. Jesus said, "I have given you an example to follow. Do as I have done to you."[10]

I wonder what would happen with the racial tension in our country if we all committed to serving our sisters. I wonder what would happen in our families if we said, "I'm going to serve my family." I wonder what would happen in our schools if we said, "I'm going to serve my teacher." I wonder what would happen in doctors' offices if we grabbed the hands of women scared to find out if they have cancer and said, "There's a God in the universe who loves you, who knows you're suffering, and who knows every hair on your head." What if we as women said, "Life is not about me, not about my agenda, and not about my dreams. Life is about being crowned to serve the King of kings and the Lord of lords." What if the fragrance of our service filled our offices, city streets, and neighborhoods?

Paul tells us, "Be alert servants of the Master, cheerfully expectant. Don't quit in hard times; pray all the harder. Help needy Christians; be inventive in hospitality" (Romans 12:11–13, MSG).

Serving is significant. When you serve, you step outside yourself. When you serve, you're saying, "God, I trust You. You walked this earth, Jesus. Your life was at risk, but You still served." He was misunderstood, but He still served. He was questioned, but He still served. He served us all the way to the cross, walking that long road with a crown of thorns on His head after being mocked, beaten, and whipped. He said, "Father, I still serve You. I'm going to cry, but I still serve You. I'm going to have to fight, but I still serve You. I'm going to serve You even unto death." But the story doesn't end there. Jesus rose from the dead so that we could have eternal life. He wore a crown of thorns to serve us, so let's serve one another. Let's get rid of the hating and say, "We're going to be those daughters. We're going to usher in a value revolution. Father God, You can have it all. We're declaring that You can take our lives, that You can breathe on us and do something miraculous in us." I dare you to worship God right now wherever you are. I dare you to praise Him. I dare you to commit to serving Him for the first time or for the hundredth time, and I know that God will fill your soul.

When you serve, your life is transformed. When you serve, miracles, signs, and wonders take place.

As God's daughters, we are crowned to serve one another. Just like Mary boldly stepped out of her comfort zone to pour out what cost her so much and serve with humility and grace.

Let's Pray

Father God, I thank You for Your presence and work in my life. I thank You that even now You're crowning me to serve. I thank You for serving me, washing me, and loving me. Help me now wash the feet of others. Jesus, I'm going to pour it all out for You. Every single thing that I have—every talent, every gift, every thought—I offer it to You. It's not about me. It's about You, Father God. I want to make Your name known. Take every single fiber of my being, Father God. Pour out Your Spirit on me. In Jesus's name.

11

CALLED TO GATHER

I'll never forget more than twenty years ago when I went to a women's conference with thousands of ladies. I had no idea what God had in store for me at that gathering of women from all over the world. I thought it was just a conference. I had no idea my life would be changed. I think heaven smiles when we gather together. It was at this conference that God spoke to my heart about leaving the broadcast news industry that I loved, asking me to join my husband in ministry. The sermon wasn't on a related topic, and if I'm honest, I don't even remember the theme of the conference. But I do remember what God spoke to my heart in that crowd of women.

As soon as I got home, I shared with my husband what God had spoken to me, and he was shocked. He had always celebrated my dreams and encouraged me to pursue them. But as I look back almost two decades later, it was one of the best decisions of my entire life. We're leading a growing, beautiful, diverse, global, life-giving church together. And every gift and skill I have, I learned from taking steps in that direction.

We're not just called to gather on a large scale like a conference. We're also called to gather in our daily lives.

I have three amazing children, and there are eleven years between the youngest and oldest. I had an elementary school kid, a middle schooler, and a high schooler all at one time. Because of their age range, I've had the opportunity to come alongside so many moms to be a mentor and big sister. No matter the season you're in, gathering with other women on similar journeys, women who have gone before you, or even women who are younger than you is a game changer. It keeps the fire burning in you, prevents you from being isolated, and helps you maintain perspective no matter how challenging the season is. In gathering, we get to find out what is considered a normal experience and ask for advice about specific situations. In gathering, we're strengthened and we grow.

We as women are often under siege. Different arrows are shot at us every single day. The world is fighting to make us forget our value, our worth, and our voice. We're under attack from the moment we're born. Girls form cliques in elementary school, already exhibiting exclusionary behavior and assigning worth based on social status. Do you ever wonder why the Enemy starts attacking women so early with comparison and jealousy? It's because of the power of gathering.

Even though women are under siege, the power of sisterhood is saying, "I'm in this with you." We're not going to conform to the world's standard of womanhood. We're not going to be like many women portrayed on reality TV shows. God bless them—they're amazing. But we're not going to be yelling at one another, pulling one another's hair, backbiting, stealing one another's husbands, and talking about one another's kids. That's not our message.

The world is also pushing us to isolate ourselves, especially when we're going through a tough time. A spirit of isolation seems to exist in our society. But it's a lying spirit. Honestly, we would never have to leave the house if we didn't want to. I'm not mad about some conveniences like Amazon Prime. I'm not mad that I can just get on my computer and Band-Aids are delivered to my door in two hours. I'm not mad that I can order groceries online, tip the driver four dollars, and avoid the commotion in a grocery store with three kids. I'm not mad about that.

But with all this convenience, the structure of our world makes us think that we don't need one another.

You can do everything from your phone. You can do everything by yourself. You can practically exist in a virtual reality. The Enemy wants the spirit of isolation to permeate our society because destructive habits form when you're alone too much. When you're alone, you feel like nobody else is hurting like you're hurting. When you're alone, you feel like your pain is the heaviest you could possibly imagine. When you're alone, you feel like you're the only one whose marriage is struggling. When you're alone, you feel like the only one who feels overweight. When you're alone, you feel like the only one who's not going to get a promotion. That's why so much power exists in the gathering of women.

Gather to Belong

We all are fighting isolation now, some more than others. Ecclesiastes 4:9–10 says, "Two people are better off than one, for they can help each other succeed. If one person falls, the other can reach out and help. But someone who falls alone is in real trouble." We're not called to be in isolation. We need physical touch, we need to lock eyes, and we need to be around one another. Community gives life. If you watch National Geographic or study animals, you know they roll deep in herds because when an animal is alone, it's vulnerable to attack. You've seen those animal documentaries where, out of the blue, a cheetah snatches a lone creature and disappears. But when herds stay tight, the predators can't attack them. So we roll deep as a sisterhood. Our gathering pushes away the Enemy.

Getting out of a dark place is much harder when you're alone. We're all going to fall. We're human, and we don't have to be perfect. You're going to fall. But the key is having someone grab your hand and say, "Girl, get back up. I know who you are. I know that you're not called to make those choices, and I'm going to pray with you until we watch that breakthrough come. We're going to go to church, we're listening to podcasts, we're going to therapy and counseling, and we're going to worship together until we cross over to victory together."

Ecclesiastes 4 has more wisdom for us: "A person standing alone can be attacked and defeated, but two can stand back-to-back and conquer. Three are even better, for a triple-braided cord is not easily broken" (verse 12). We are women who are not easily broken because we are women who can say, "I'm a part of a sisterhood. I'm a part of a triple-braided cord."

Your finances aren't going to break you. Your relationships aren't going to break you. Your fears aren't going to break you. Your insecurities aren't going to break you. Because you will be supported and encouraged in the sisterhood. We all find belonging when we allow ourselves to live in community with the beautiful and messy people God's placed around us. We're called to gather.

The world is getting dark. But a companion can help you bear the darkness and carry the weight of the world. We come together to give one another hope and to speak life. We don't have to have it all together. I sure don't. As I write this chapter, my toes aren't even polished! I don't remember the last time I had a pedicure. I haven't had time. Don't get me one. Really, I don't need you to get me one. But if you were to look closely at my toes, you would think, *Bless her.*

Jesus shows up when we gather.

But here's the deal: we don't have to have it all together.

One of my weeks a few years ago was really crazy. Earl had knee surgery so that he can dunk more because he loves basketball and also so that he can run around with our kids. In the previous chapter, I talked about being crowned to serve. Well, I earned a couple of crowns that week as I ran around to make sure Earl had everything he needed. I even asked him, "Do you feel I'm doing a good job?" Because you know how you sometimes can feel like you've taken care of someone well, but they still need more? Part of you might think, *Wow, okay. I guess I don't have anything to do but serve you.* I'm just being honest. So I said, "Earl, do you feel taken care of? Do you feel like I'm leaning into you? Do you feel good?" And he said, "Yes, you've been amazing." I was so relieved! That was a crazy week. But I knew that if I could just get to church and be surrounded by the sisterhood of all my girls and if I could just sit in God's presence, God would meet me there, and He absolutely did. I know that He's meeting you right now too.

You don't have to do life alone.

From Earl's knee surgery to sending my oldest child to college, I wouldn't have survived without community. Meals, encouraging texts, advice from other moms who have launched their kids—all of this has buffered this season with grace and strength. I'm passionate about this: *You don't have to go it alone.*

Sadly, many of us have been hurt in community and are afraid to trust again. I first want to say I'm so sorry for the pain you've experienced—it makes sense why you want to skip this chapter. But can I tell you I've been hurt too? I've been misunderstood. I've been betrayed by friends who I thought would never turn their back on me. I prayed and allowed God to heal my broken heart. Was it awful? Yes. Was it hard? Yes. But I will tell you God has healed my heart. Though it did take time. I decided I'm going to love big and trust again and allow new friends and healed friends to surround me. I say all this to say that when we're surrounded by the right healthy people, we're strengthened, encouraged, and able to make it through almost anything.

Gather in the Good and Bad Times

We're called to gather when we're burning in the furnace of trouble. When the heat is turned up, we're still called to come together.

When fire's coming from everywhere and we think, *Could this situation possibly get any worse? Could the fire possibly get any hotter? Could life possibly get any more difficult?*—guess what? We're still called to gather. In the good times and in the bad.

In the book of Exodus, we get a fascinating look at the power of women working shoulder to shoulder during the time when Israel was enslaved to Egypt:

> Pharaoh, the king of Egypt, gave this order to the Hebrew midwives, Shiphrah and Puah: "When you help the Hebrew women as they give birth, watch as they deliver. If the baby is a boy, kill him; if it is a girl, let her live." But because the midwives feared God, they refused to obey the king's orders. They allowed the boys to live, too.
>
> So the king of Egypt called for the midwives. "Why have you done this?" he demanded. "Why have you allowed the boys to live?"
>
> "The Hebrew women are not like the Egyptian women," the midwives replied. "They are more vigorous and have their babies so quickly that we cannot get there in time."
>
> So God was good to the midwives, and the Israelites continued to multiply, growing more and more powerful. And because the midwives feared God, he gave them families of their own. (1:15–21)

I love how these two midwives used their position to protect the next generation. They didn't let the king stop them from being used by God. That is so powerful. Who are you supposed to gather with at your job, at your school, in your neighborhood? Don't underestimate the power of gathering.

There's a plan and a purpose for every woman created. We're reminding the women of the world that God hasn't forgotten about them and that He will never leave them or forsake them.[1] That is the power of sisterhood. That is the power of gathering. Together, we push against the current.

When others judge, we love.

When others gossip, we speak life.

When others ignore, we lean in.

We are that sisterhood. We are those girls. Speak this over yourself: "I'm that girl."

When you understand the power of a gathering of women, you'll be expectant about what God can do in your life, what miracles He can do on your behalf, and what battles He can fight. An old African proverb says, "If you want to go fast, go alone. But if you want to go far, go together." We as a sisterhood go together. We're going to go farther. We're not alone. We're for one another. We believe in one another. We speak life into one another. We're one another's cheerleaders. You can cheer in a skirt or combat boots as long as you're cheering for somebody. We believe that we're called to do exceedingly abundantly more than we could ever ask, think, or imagine.[2] But we can't let one another make the journey alone; we need to say, "You know what? I'm going with you." If you're reading this, we're in this life together. You're not alone.

Gather with the Presence

Finally, Matthew 18:20 says, "Where two or three gather in my name, there am I with them" (NIV). God is here right now with you, He is here in your storm, and He is here to bring break-through. Whatever fire you're facing, whatever storm, I'm believing that heaven is going to invade earth on your behalf.

We come from a long line of women who gathered with purpose and power. Deborah and Jael double-teamed the enemy and took him down. And as we saw in the last chapter, Mary Magdalene, Joanna, Susanna, and many other women helped fund Jesus's ministry.[3] I think about the women who gathered around the tomb to prepare Jesus's body for burial. All throughout Scripture, we see how when women gather together, God shows up. Hebrews 12 tells us that we're surrounded by a cloud of witnesses and urges us to throw off everything that hinders and entangles us.[4] When we gather together, we help one another throw down weights that would try to hold us back.

If you've had trouble finding an amazing church or healthy community, I encourage you to start a neighborhood or online Bible study. Maybe consider starting an office Bible study or work-out group. If you're in school, consider asking a few girls to work out with you or do a book study together. You can form the community you're craving. Another great way to meet people is to volunteer in your community. You will be surprised by the women you meet outside your comfort zone.

Let's Pray

Father God, I thank You that even when I walk through tough times, Your presence is with me to strengthen me and encourage me. I thank You that chains are falling right now, that hope is coming right now, that peace is flooding my heart, that miracles are being performed in my finances, my mind, and my body. I thank You that Your presence surrounds me and reminds me that I am not alone, even in the fire.

12

BE STILL IN THE MIDDLE

When you see me smiling with my son Grayson, you might assume that we never had to fight for anything. You might not know that we adopted him. You might not know that we cried out to God for two and a half years for him to come into our lives. When Earl and I met in college, we knew we wanted to have biological children, but we also had a heart for adoption. We waited seven years until our first baby was born. We were just enjoying that newlywed life, being spontaneous. It was fun. No rush. Then we had our oldest, Parker. A few years after having Parker, we thought, *You know what? It's probably time for baby number two.* But we thought, *Let's adopt instead of having another biological baby.* So we went to the adoption agency and sat through the orientation classes, where they told us, "Oh, you'll have a baby in four to six months." Two and a half years later, we were in our middle. Most people don't know this part of our story. We got paired up with three different birth moms. Each time, we were expectant, thinking that they had picked us to be the parents. We thought we were finally having a little girl, who we were going to name Grace. That's why Grayson's name is Grayson. He was supposed to be Grace, but God had other plans.

We would be paired with these birth moms, they would look through our adoption book, and then our adoption agent would call us to say, "You've been picked." We would get so excited and tell all our friends. Then we would get a call after four weeks that the birth mom had decided to go a different direction. This happened three times. We felt like we had this promise in our hearts— this dream to adopt—but every time we were chosen, then rejected, we felt like we had experienced a miscarriage. Finally, the adoption agency said they had a girl for us, so Earl was on cloud nine. We were waiting to find out when we could go pick up our little girl. All my girlfriends had planned a baby shower for me and had picked out bedding for her room. I bought a journal with the name Grace written on it. The nursery was going to be decorated in florals and stripes and was going to be beautiful. At Parker's preschool graduation, I told Earl, "Today the adoption agency is going to call us to tell us that Grace has been born and that we can go pick her up." Then the phone rang, and I stepped outside the classroom to hear sadness in the voice of the adoption counselor. She said, "The birth mom actually decided to go with the family that previously adopted another one of her children." We went from this high of thinking that we were about to pick up our little girl to feeling so discouraged because this was the third time that our dreams and hopes had been shattered. I'll never forget thinking, *God, where are You in this? You're the one who placed this seed in our hearts to have a little girl. Where are You? I thought You were fighting this battle for us.*

We were super discouraged. We just got in the car, went home, packed our bags, drove to Dallas, and found a hotel. As we were driving, Earl looked at me as the city skyline came into view and said, "I wonder if we're supposed to plant a church there." In the midst of our brokenness, in the midst of us feeling as if God had deserted us, in the middle of our battle, He planted a dream in our hearts for the church that we lead today. But that dream was accompanied by struggle and some tears. I just want to tell you that, in the middle of whatever you're facing, God can show up and plant dreams and visions in your heart.

Sometimes it's easy to believe that God is the Alpha and Omega, the beginning and end, but we forget that He's God even in the middle.

In the middle of your worst days, He's still God.

In the middle of your doubt, He's still God.

In the middle of your fears, He's still God.

He can show up in any situation.

Revelation 1:8 says, "The Master declares, 'I'm A to Z. I'm THE GOD WHO IS, THE GOD WHO WAS, AND THE GOD ABOUT TO ARRIVE'" (MSG). Do you need God to arrive in a situation that you're facing? Do you need to be reminded that He's going to show up, that He's on time, and that He's going to provide for you? He's faithful, He's true, and He's still on the scene fighting for you and me. We sometimes do ourselves a disservice because we talk about God being the Alpha when our lives are peaceful or we give Him praise at the end of a trial when we can see Him as the Omega. But He's still God even when things aren't great.

There are some critical, supernatural middle moments in Scripture. God did this on purpose so that when life gets hard, we'll know we can trust His faithfulness.

John 19:17-18 says, "They took Jesus, therefore, and He went out, carrying His own cross, to the place called the Place of a Skull, which in Hebrew is called, Golgotha. There they crucified Him, and with Him two other men, one on either side, and Jesus in between" (NASB). He's been in the middle. Jesus knows the pain and struggle you feel when you're in the middle, hard-pressed on every side. God can show up in the middle of our mess. He can show up when we're lost.

I'll never forget that drive with Earl. We didn't say much to each other, because no words could communicate our feelings. We were heartbroken and downtrodden. But we didn't know that God was working behind the scenes, using that situation to plant a city in our hearts and to get us the child who we were called to love—our little boy Grayson.

We returned from that trip with a dream to plant a church in Dallas. Then, a few months later, we found out that Grayson was already growing in his birth mother's womb during the time we were feeling forgotten. Our son was being prepared for us. We had no idea. I'll never forget calling our adoption agency, saying, "My heart keeps getting broken in a million pieces, so I'm done being paired with birth moms. Just call me when you have a baby." Earl thought that was harsh, but I said, "I can't take it anymore. Just call me when you have a baby." I'll never forget the day the phone rang and the agency said, "We have an eight-pound baby boy for you," and our lives were forever wrecked by him.

God tells us, "Be still, and know that I am God; I will be exalted among the nations, I will be exalted in the earth" (Psalm 46:10, NIV). This means that the journey to bring Grayson home wasn't over until God was exalted. This means that you can be still because He's got the fight. He's fighting this battle for you. You have to rest in His presence. You have to accept the peace with which He wants to clothe you. Don't be fighting with the wind, wrestling with nothing, and stressing yourself out. Just be still and rest, especially in the middle of the journey, knowing that He's got you covered.

Your journey isn't over until God is exalted.

I love Psalm 55, where David cried out to God with some very real problems. He was literally running for his life, and he had been betrayed, just to name a few of the challenges he was facing. He wrote, "I call to God; GOD will help me. At dusk, dawn, and noon I sigh deep sighs—he hears, he rescues. My life is well and whole, secure in the middle of danger even while thousands are lined up against me" (verses 16–18, MSG). At dusk, at dawn, and at noon, David was crying out. He was desperate. His heart was hurting. But he knew that God hears and God rescues. I want to tell you that God hears your cry and He is going to rescue you. In the very next line, David said, "My life is well and whole." We have to remember this when we're in the middle, feeling forgotten or lost. Maybe we feel like God is no longer God or that He isn't going to intervene, but David got it right. He said in hope, "My life is well and whole." When you're in the middle of something, I dare you to say, "All hell is breaking loose in my life, but I am well and whole because I am in the middle of His will. I'm secure." David was in the middle of danger with thousands lined up against him, yet it was well with his soul. David was in the middle, but he knew that God was with him.

It's important for us to know that our Father isn't afraid to be with us in our mess.

He's not afraid of the dirt.

He's not afraid of the crazy.

He's not afraid of your temper.

He's not afraid of your shortcomings.

He's not afraid of your sharp tongue.

He's not afraid of your boss at work.

He's still with you. He's waiting to show Himself faithful on your behalf. God's right there just waiting for you to grab His hand through all your struggle.

When we're in the middle, God calls us to be still and stand firm. To be still means to remain in place and at rest, motionless.[1] That means you're not blowing up everybody's phone in a panic, not ranting on social media, not sending hate mail, but just being still. To be still also means to be "free from sound or noise."[2] Silent. At peace, even in the middle. Your mind might be racing with thoughts like, *But wait, God! I need to tell them because they need to know how I feel. I need to fight this myself, God. They need to know. I need to show up. I need to stand up. Who's going to fight for me?* Just be still.

In some seasons, God wakes up the fight inside you. In other seasons, He says, "Don't fight; let Me fight for you." Sometimes we put on our gloves to get in the ring. Other times we don't have the energy to get out of bed. And when that happens, you can find rest in your Father.

Just be still.

"You will not even need to fight," says 2 Chronicles 20:17.

When we're in the middle of a battle, our tendency is to jump in and fight it ourselves, which is just human nature. But that's not God's nature. The verse goes on to say, "Take your positions; then stand still and watch the LORD's victory. He is with you, O people of Judah and Jerusalem. Do not be afraid or discouraged. Go out against them tomorrow, for the LORD is with you!" The Lord of hosts is with you. God and His angel armies are fighting this battle for you. So you're not showing up to this battle alone. God isn't saying, "Don't come to the battle. Stay at home. Put your head under a pillow, and hide." He's gangster. He says, "Come. Put on your full armor. Come to the battle. Come to the fight. Come to the front lines, and watch Me as I fight on your behalf. Watch Me fight this battle for you. Watch Me slay these giants. Come. Come expectant. Don't chase the battle. Just stay still. Be battle ready and show up."

Show up in your marriage, even when it's hard.

Show up to your job on those days when you think, *Really? Really? They're going to ask me to do that again, really?*

Show up for your friends who need you.

Show up to church when you're in the middle of something.

When we show up, we see God work. He says, "Be present, be alert, but stand still." We don't have to carry the weight of the battle on our own shoulders. This is such good news. We don't have to do life by ourselves. He's with us.

Exodus 14 tells us how the children of Israel were trapped on every side. They couldn't escape the Red Sea in front of them and the Egyptian army behind them. But Moses told the people, "Do not be afraid. Stand still, and see the salvation of the LORD, which He will accomplish for you today" (verse 13, NKJV). Anticipate that God is going to show up, and be expectant about what He will do, not what He might do. The passage continues, "The LORD will fight for you, and you shall hold your peace" (verse 14, NKJV). If you feel trapped with no escape possible, God is saying, "I've got you. Just stand, be still, and rest in knowing that I'm going to fight this for you. You do not have to fight it yourself."

> *Be expectant about what He*
> *will do, not what He might do.*

He hasn't forgotten you. Your circumstances right now are setting you up for your future. The battle is a setup for His light to shine. It's a setup for His peace to fill your heart. It's a setup for Him to get the glory and the honor and the praise. But you have to stand, you have to be still, and you have to let Him fight for you. Get out of the fight because victory is already yours. God claimed victory for every single thing we would ever face when He died on the cross. He didn't say life was going to be easy. But He did say, "I've come to fight for you. I've come to overcome, and I've come to bring life."

Ephesians 6:10–13 says, "Be strong in the Lord and in his mighty power. Put on the full armor of God, so that you can take your stand against the devil's schemes. For our struggle is not against flesh and blood, but against the rulers, against the authorities, against the powers of this dark world and against the spiritual forces of evil in the heavenly realms. Therefore put on the full armor of God, so that when the day of evil comes, you may be able to stand your ground, and after you have done everything, to stand" (NIV).

The struggle is not against your spouse. It's not against your boss. It's not against your co-workers. It's not against your family.

Stand your ground. If you get that unexpected phone call, if you get that unexpected text message, if you get fired or broken up with, stand. Stand. He's going to fight this battle for you. He's going to win this battle for you.

The Bible offers such strength to us: "Thanks be to God! He gives us the victory through our Lord Jesus Christ. Therefore, my dear brothers and sisters, stand firm. Let nothing move you. Always give yourselves fully to the work of the Lord, because you know that your labor in the Lord is not in vain" (1 Corinthians 15:57–58, NIV).

And we have this encouragement too: "Let us not become weary in doing good, for at the proper time we will reap a harvest if we do not give up" (Galatians 6:9, NIV).

What are you in the middle of right now? I want to tell you that our God is faithful to do exceedingly abundantly more than you could ever ask, think, or imagine.[3] I challenge you to stand still in your middle until He shows up.

Let's Pray

Father God, I am Your daughter; You see me. I thank

You that You are changing the atmosphere around me

right now. I thank You that Your presence is with me. I

thank You that You are transforming my life, and I pray that You would give me the strength that I need to stand, no matter what I'm facing. I pray that You would fight every battle for me, that You would renew my mind, and that You would strengthen me from the inside out. God, please show up in my life, show up in my family, show up in my job, show up in my body, and show up in my city. I thank You for the revival taking place in me. Thank You that, even in the middle, even in the waiting, even in the preparation, You are still God.

13

WORSHIP IN THE BATTLE

When we find ourselves in the middle of a battle or facing an impossible situation, God equips us with a surprising tool. That's what Jehoshaphat learned, and it's what we need to learn too.

Jehoshaphat became the king of Judah and within a few years found himself in an impossible situation. Second Chronicles 20 tells us, "The Moabites and Ammonites with some of the Meunites came to wage war against Jehoshaphat. Some people came and told Jehoshaphat, 'A vast army is coming against you from Edom. . . .'" Alarmed, Jehoshaphat resolved to inquire of the LORD, and he proclaimed a fast for all Judah" (verses 1–3, NIV).

Do you ever feel like life is just waging war against you? Jehoshaphat felt like this. A vast army was coming against him. I love the word *resolved* here. In his fear, in his moment of feeling like, *What the what? It just got real,* it's like he said to himself, "I'm not going to let this battle crush me. I may feel a little shaken right now, but I'm going to be strong in faith." He found courage to say, "I'm not going to fight this in my flesh, so let's fast." To fast is to give up something. You have to die to yourself and to the way you want to accomplish or fix things. That's what Jehoshaphat did. He said, "I can't fight this battle by myself. I'm going to call a fast for everybody so that we can seek the face of God." Picture this: He was in the courtyard with all the people of his kingdom. Every man, woman, and child was represented. God wanted even the children, who were Judah's next generation, to see how people should roll when they're in the middle. The enemy was marching toward them and wasn't stopping, but they turned to the Lord. I love this.

Then Jehoshaphat stood up before the crowd and said, "LORD, the God of our ancestors, are you not the God who is in heaven? You rule over all the kingdoms of the nations. Power and might are in your hand, and no one can withstand you" (verse 6, NIV).

Sometimes we have to remind ourselves—and everyone watching—who God is. We have to say, "Father God, I thank You that You're God of this situation. I thank You that You're still on the throne. I thank You that You own the kingdoms and that You know the beginning and the end. You're the Alpha and Omega even while I'm facing impossible odds." Even though Jehoshaphat was fearful, he didn't want the situation to overwhelm him. So he reminded himself and all his people of the One who was still on the throne.

Jehoshaphat continued praying: "We have no power to face this vast army that is attacking us. We do not know what to do, but our eyes are on you" (verse 12, NIV). I love that Jehoshaphat was honest about the situation. He didn't pretend he knew what the next steps were but admitted he had no clue what to do. Because he was a young king, he could've thought he needed to prove to everyone that he was competent, that he had this figured out. But he was honest and humble. He didn't let pride get in the way. We shouldn't either. It's okay if we don't know what to do. Jehoshaphat said, "Our eyes are on you." Whatever you're battling, keep your eyes on God. Don't stare at the situation. Put your focus on Him, and He will give you the clarity that you need to walk the situation out.

This next part gets exciting. The Holy Spirit settled on Jahaziel, and he said to all the people gathered there, "Do not be afraid or discouraged because of this vast army. For the battle is not yours, but God's. . . . You will not have to fight this battle. Take up your positions; stand firm and see the deliverance the LORD will give you, Judah and Jerusalem. Do not be afraid; do not be discouraged. Go out to face them tomorrow, and the LORD will be with you" (verses 15, 17, NIV).

In the middle of the crisis, the Spirit of the Lord spoke through a Levite. His declaration was spontaneous. Jehoshaphat didn't instruct Jahaziel to jump up with a speech to bring peace. God moved Jahaziel to speak a prophetic word. The interesting thing is, Jahaziel's name means "beheld by God."[1] I don't think that was accidental. I think that the Spirit of the living God flooded that place to remind them that each one of them was beheld by God.

I'm believing that you will come to know that you are beheld by God. God knows you. God knows *you*. How comforting that is.

After hearing God's words spoken through Jahaziel, Jehoshaphat bowed down, and all the people of Judah, too, their faces on the ground before the Lord. And they praised God with loud shouts.

Instead of letting fear override the situation, the people worshipped God. Sometimes, when the battle's raging against us, we have to speak to the situation and let it know that this battle isn't going to take us out. Sometimes, when negative thoughts come against our minds, we have to start worshipping and praising God, saying, "God, I'm not going to let these thoughts override Your promises." That's what the people of Judah did.

> *God sees you. He knows every battle that you're fighting, and He is holding you.*

The people of Judah fought in a different way: They fasted and worshipped. God has called us as Christians not to fight like the world but to fight in a different way. Paul wrote in 2 Corinthians, "The weapons of our warfare are not of the flesh, but divinely powerful for the destruction of fortresses. We are destroying arguments and all arrogance raised against the knowledge of God, and we are taking every thought captive to the obedience of Christ" (10:4–5, NASB). I love that. We're taking every thought captive, meaning that we're bringing every thought under control. Thoughts like, *It will always be this way; I'm not good enough; I can't provide for my family; I'm going to lose my house; I'm going to lose my husband; I'm going to lose who I am as a person.* Don't entertain those thoughts by taking them out to dinner and a movie. Stop those thoughts by saying, "You're under arrest, ill thought. You don't have any place in my mind. Right now, I'm taking you captive, and I'm going to let Christ renew my mind."

Sometimes those thoughts come like bullets out of the blue.

You could be worshipping, and an intrusive thought will flash into your mind. Has that ever happened to you? It's happened to me. Thoughts will come out of nowhere, just shot right at you. But you know what you have to do? You have to take every thought captive, and you need to say, "You don't belong here." Sometimes, when I'm angry at the devil or a situation and my thoughts are plaguing me, I'll literally just lay hands on my head and say, "Thank You, God, that I have the mind of Christ. Thank You that no weapon formed against me shall prosper." Sometimes you just have to lay hands on yourself.

Taking every thought captive isn't a normal protocol when you're in crisis mode, because you feel like you need to fight the battle yourself or defend yourself. But even Jehoshaphat didn't do that. He went straight to God. This was his battle strategy, and this should be our battle strategy also.

You would think that Jehoshaphat's next action would be rolling out a map on a table and saying, "Okay, I'm going to place soldiers here, here, and here." But he didn't do that, because our weapons aren't carnal. Instead, Jehoshaphat "appointed singers to walk ahead of the army, singing to the LORD and praising him for his holy splendor" (2 Chronicles 20:21).

The battle plan wasn't based on having a bigger army, but it was based on worshipping God in the battle, singing out despite the situation, and saying, "God, You are good, and Your love endures forever. You are going to get us through this situation."

While the army marched behind the singers praising God, "the LORD set ambushes against the men of Ammon and Moab and Mount Seir who were invading Judah, and they were defeated" (verse 22, NIV). Can you imagine what the singers were thinking when they were sent to the front lines not to wield weapons but to worship God? But while they were worshipping, God set ambushes. The Spirit of the living God sent confusion into the enemy's camp, and they started fighting one another instead of Jehoshaphat and his people.

Jehoshaphat's battle plan was worship. We're going to learn to worship our way through the battle, because if it worked for Jehoshaphat, it will work for us.

It's one thing to worship when life is good. It's another thing to worship when you pick up the phone to find out your best friend has cancer. It's another thing to worship when you find out your son is lost and you don't know where he is. It's another thing to worship when you get a bad report from the doctor or you feel like your marriage is falling apart. But we're supposed to worship in the troubling times when everything in our lives seems to be falling apart. Do you believe me? Because if you do, you're going to see God set ambushes against oncoming attackers.

Verse 30 says, "The kingdom of Jehoshaphat was at peace, for his God had given him rest on every side" (NIV). God gave him rest on his right, his left, and in the front and back. God gave him peace through worship. This is so powerful and such good news.

When my older son, Parker, was in elementary school, he told me that, during worship in the kids' ministry, he saw a vision. He said, "While I was worshipping, I saw myself standing and speaking before people." He had never talked like this before. He usually told us that he wanted to be a basketball player or whatever other profession was popular with his friends at the time. But that day he told me, with a sweet, tender spirit, that he had been called to the ministry while worshipping God. Earl and I started to cry. We said, "No matter what you do with your life, we love you and we believe in you." But it was in an atmosphere of worship that Parker saw himself in the future. Right after church that particular day (I didn't know that any of this had happened), he said, "Mom, will you take me into the church's auditorium?" So I did. The auditorium was mostly empty, and he just looked and walked around. He later told me that his vision had compelled him to walk around the auditorium because he had seen himself speaking in front of crowds. God will give you visions for your future while you worship.

I remember another time when worship factored into our family's story. When our younger son, Grayson, was five years old, he was lost on the school bus during his first week of school. They dropped him off in the wrong neighborhood. Yeah, it was a really crazy, terrible day. We found him, but Earl and I were broken, frustrated, and discouraged because our little boy was lost. After hugging him tightly, then dealing with the principal and the school, we fell to our knees; we walked into our bedroom and just started worshipping God because we didn't know what else to do. Peace flooded our hearts in that moment.

Recently, we had a funeral at Shoreline City for a sweet little four-year-old boy. So many people from our church prayed and worshipped in the chapel of the hospital while his family was in the middle of their son's fight for his life. Our people's praise and worship touched others in the hospital because worship was surrounding this family's struggle. Before the funeral, his beautiful mom and I were in an upstairs room of the church, and she gazed out the window, watching the cars arrive. Then one of her little boys started bawling because he was going to miss his brother. Do you know what she did? She grabbed him and sang over him. Even in her darkest pain, she knew worship was the only thing that was going to get her through. If we can grasp this concept, peace can flood every situation in our lives.

At the funeral, the worship team sang "How Great Is Our God,"[2] and that song changed the atmosphere. Before they started singing, the atmosphere was heavy with aching, longing, and brokenness; we were all crying. But then the team started singing, "How great is our God! Sing with me, how great is our God." Suddenly, the Spirit of the living God rose up and ministered peace. I'm here to tell you that worship will change the atmosphere, set ambushes for oncoming attackers, and destroy strongholds.

Worship changes the atmosphere, sets ambushes for oncoming attackers, and destroys strongholds.

One of my favorite scriptures is found in Isaiah:

> The Spirit of the Lord GOD is upon Me,
> Because the LORD has anointed Me
> To preach good tidings to the poor;
> He has sent Me to heal the brokenhearted,
> To proclaim liberty to the captives,
> And the opening of the prison to those who are bound;

To proclaim the acceptable year of the LORD,

And the day of vengeance of our God;

To comfort all who mourn,

To console those who mourn in Zion,

To give them beauty for ashes,

The oil of joy for mourning,

The garment of praise for the spirit of heaviness;

That they may be called trees of righteousness,

The planting of the LORD, that He may be glorified.

(61:1–3, NKJV)

I'm believing that if you're feeling heavy, God is going to wrap you in a garment of praise in exchange for your spirit of heaviness. I'm believing that God in the Spirit is going to transfer the weight of what you're feeling and drape you in praise.

I worship when I'm on the mountaintop and when I'm in the lowest valley. I worship because my soul needs it. I worship because it reminds me that God is on the throne and bigger than any battle I face. I worship to renew my mind, purify my heart, help my perspective, and keep me sane. It's amazing how locking eyes with Jesus, thanking Him for what He has done and is going to do, pushes back darkness and refreshes our souls. I've sung over my teenager's room; I've sung over my little girl's room. I've even blasted worship music from the front seat of an ambulance after receiving life-threatening news about my husband. I'm sure the driver was like, *What is this girl doing?* but I didn't care. In my desperation, I invited God's presence to fill me up for the battle we were facing.

I don't know what you or your family are in the middle of, but I believe, by the Spirit of God, that He's going to wrap you in the mantle of His presence. I don't know what battles rage in your community and beyond, but I dare you to worship, and I dare you to lift your hands to heaven and say, "Not my will, but Your will be done." I'm declaring that you can bless the Lord at all times, that God will meet you wherever you are, and that His Spirit will cover you.

Let's Pray

Dear Jesus, by faith I lift my hands to heaven in this moment, and I commit to worshipping You even before the victory. I remind myself in this moment that You are still worthy of my praise. Just like Paul and Silas worshipped in chains, I'm going to worship in the midst of my pain and my circumstances. You are on the throne, and I thank You for Your faithfulness, goodness, and kindness in the middle of every storm. I thank You for fighting battles on my behalf, and I thank You that You are bigger than any challenge I face. You are worthy; You are holy. I exalt You and You alone.

14

YOUR WORD IS YES

I remember when one of my sons was going through the terrible twos. I call him "our spirited one" to gently characterize his craziness, but he was a hot mess. He'd break down and throw tantrums when we'd go out. We'd try to pick him up, but he'd be dead weight. Can any parents identify? Sometimes God is calling us to say yes, but we're kicking and screaming along the way. Let's stop the dead-weight drop! When God says yes to your calling, say yes also. When God says yes to the plans He has for you, say yes. When God says yes to your beauty, value, and worth, you have to agree with His yes. Our yes plus His yes is powerful!

God has called us to say a confident yes. The Word says that Christ within us is the hope of glory.[1] We're stamped with His Spirit. Our surety in Christ is what gives us the power to say yes. You don't have to rely on your own power—tap into His! God already said yes for you when He allowed His Son to die for you on the cross. So, when you say yes to a new season and when you say yes to God's plan for your future, you're saying amen to what He has already said. Imagine what would happen if we all said yes. Imagine the ramifications of thousands of our yeses. Imagine the power of thousands of us realizing that God has chosen us to be that girl, part of a plan that is unfolding in heaven. It's time for us to get a little bit uncomfortable and prepare to be challenged, because God is calling us to a season of yes. He wants to push us forward. The seat you're sitting in right now is a launching pad into your destiny. I don't want you to think that you're just sitting on a living room couch, because you're really at mission control and God is about to count down: "Three, two, one."

Many times our yes starts with questions. I think about Mary in the gospel of Luke right before she went to visit her cousin Elizabeth. An angel had just appeared to Mary and told her that she was about to become pregnant and bring forth the Savior of the world. Can you imagine being engaged, not married yet, and an angel just shows up and tells you that you're about to be pregnant with the Savior? Of course, Mary immediately questioned the word she had been given: "Mary said to the angel, 'But how? I've never slept with a man'" (1:34, MSG). Sometimes our "But how?" keeps us from stepping into the yes of God's calling, because we like to figure out the process first.

Here's the deal: God is waiting for us on the other side of our yes. However, sometimes our "But how?" will lock down our action. God is saying, "I want to unlock what's inside you, even before you understand what I am doing." If He told us what was going to happen, if He told us His full plan, we wouldn't be able to handle it, because it's too great. So let's not have a questioning spirit. Of course, we can ask questions because God welcomes our humanity and takes our questions seriously. But let's stop waiting on another and another word from the Lord before we move into action when we know He is inviting us to step fully into the life He has called us to.

Sometimes Earl will plan a date on our day off and won't want to tell me what we're doing, but I like to know the plan. Sometimes he'll surprise me and say, "I'm going to take you on a date, and it's going to be an adventure." But I start asking so many questions that I can't enjoy the journey. Of course, it's natural at times to have questions. But our questions can hold us back. Our "But how?" can act as our brakes. God is saying, "Stop questioning. Stop trying to figure everything out. Stop trying to chart everything. Stop trying to make grids and graphs and checklists." Just say yes, and He'll give you grace for the future. Stop asking "How?" We keep waiting for the "How," but He is waiting on our yes, then will show us the "How" in His time.

> *Mary moved from "How" to "Yes." And we can too.*

By the end of Mary's conversation with the angel, she said, "Yes, I see it all now: I'm the Lord's maid, ready to serve" (verse 38, MSG). God is calling us to have that posture too.

But as I've learned in my life, there are many ways to say yes.

The Fully Persuaded Yes

Romans 4:19–21 says this about Abraham after God promised him a son: "Without weakening in his faith, he acknowledged the decrepitness of his body (since he was about a hundred years old) and the lifelessness of Sarah's womb. Yet he did not waver through disbelief in the promise of God, but was strengthened in his faith and gave glory to God, being fully persuaded that God was able to do what He had promised" (BSB). Abraham didn't waver, which means that he didn't go back and forth with thoughts such as, *Well, maybe I'm called, and maybe I'm not. Well, maybe God has a plan for my family, and maybe He doesn't. Well, maybe my future's in His hands, and maybe it's not.* No— Abraham was fully persuaded on the good days and the bad days.

We need to go back to the Word and be fully persuaded that He will never leave us or forsake us,[2] that He has plans for our lives,[3] that He knows every single hair on our heads.[4] He wants us to be fully persuaded in our yes.

Abraham was fully persuaded. I want us running into what God has for us with the fierce posture of a lion, not the fear and timidity of a turtle. Be fully persuaded even if you don't fully understand yet.

The Unselfish Yes

I also call this one "the big-girl yes." This type of yes involves no benefit to you. It ensures another person's blessing because of you. The unselfish yes is a more mature version of yes. This yes pays for someone else to go to dinner, and you watch them eat but don't taste it yourself. Moses's mother placed him in the Nile and didn't get to enjoy him in her home, because he was adopted by the pharaoh's daughter.[5] Her yes made a way for Moses to change a generation. It's possible she didn't get to watch him crawl on the floor of her little house, and she didn't get to see him take his first steps. But her yes caused a ripple effect that we look to for inspiration today. She said a big-girl yes, and I believe that God is calling us to step into this type of yes. My middle child, Grayson, came into our lives because a young woman, probably nineteen or twenty years old, realized that she couldn't give him the life he needed. She went through the very selfless process of putting together an adoption plan for him. Can you imagine? Maybe you've placed a child for adoption. You felt the baby kick, went to the doctor's appointments, watched the ultrasounds, and dreamed about your child's future. But then the realization hit you that you're never going to get to watch him take his first step, never going to get to take him out to ice cream or put money under his pillow when he loses a tooth. I'll never forget when we walked into this young lady's hospital room. We met her when Grayson was just three days old. She began to tell us her story, and Earl just looked at her and said, "You are so brave." Her yes has changed our family. Her yes brought this beautiful little boy, who we are madly in love with, into our home. As a result of her unselfish yes, Grayson is growing up in love with Jesus and planted in God's house. God is calling you to an unselfish yes. Although you might not get to enjoy the fruit of your yes, you know and find peace that it's making a way for someone else.

My mother-in-law, Diane, was a single mom raising a little boy in the inner city. She worked two jobs and faced so much adversity, but she kept showing up and serving in church, kept exposing Earl to church, kept saying yes when it was tough, kept saying yes when she didn't know how the bills were going to be paid, kept saying yes without a husband, and kept saying yes to her son's dreams. Because she said yes, I'm now married to my very best friend and I get to spend my life with him. I want to honor her yes.

The Pioneering Yes

This is the type of yes where you say yes before anybody else. It's easy to say, "Oh yeah, me too," when everybody else has already said yes. Sometimes that's okay. But maybe God is calling you to say a pioneering yes to something that's never been done before. He might be calling you to step out and say yes before something is popular or before others do. This type of yes makes me think of my pastors, Rob and Laura Koke. Laura, who I mentioned earlier, is my mentor and dear friend. She is a pioneering-yes kind of woman. She and Rob have said yes to more than thirty-five years of ministry at their church, Shoreline Austin. She has said yes to late nights, phone calls, text messages, being believed in, being stabbed in the back, and building a church that ten thousand people are now attending. She has said yes to pouring into and mentoring me. It's one thing to feel like you've done well when you've said yes for two years. If you've invested only a short amount of time, you might think, *Check me out! Look at my followers. Look at my feed.* But try saying yes for more than three decades, no matter the struggle or heartache involved. I love my pastors so much and am so grateful for their yes.

Laura and Rob walked through a tragedy several years ago when their son Caleb passed away. Laura could have opted out of her yes. She could have said, "I get a pass in life because I'm walking through one of the most tragic events that a parent could ever have to face." But she didn't say no even though no one would have judged her for it. Her yes actually got louder in the face of her adversity. I dare you to keep your yes strong like hers even in the face of trouble. Now her yes is being felt all over the world.

Laura's yes made a way for my yes. Your yes isn't just about you. It's about the next generation. Your legacy doesn't end when your life does. Others are supposed to carry out what you start. Your yes can have a domino effect, leading to yes after yes after yes. I need you to wake up. I need you to step into what God has called you to, because He's saying right now, "Daughter, rise up; step into My plans and purposes. Don't hold back. Stop thinking about yourself, and think about who's going to be affected by your yes."

Your yes is going to make a way for somebody else's yes.

The Enduring Yes

We might be called to say yes to things that we won't even see come to fruition in our lifetime. But we want to be women who leave a legacy through the yeses that we say.

Years ago, many women prayed for a revolution like this. They never got to see a generation of women saying yes to God's calling on their lives and saying yes to sisterhood. They prayed for a time when they could look to their right and left and see Black women, Hispanic women, white women, Asian women, and Indigenous women all worshipping Jesus Christ, the King of kings and the Lord of lords. Those women paid the price so that we could experience a value revolution with our yes. Those women probably walked into their prayer closets and prayed, "Father God, I believe that one day there will be revival among women of a future generation. I believe that one day women of all backgrounds will worship Your name together." We stand on the foundation of the many prayers of the women who came before us. The prayers of those women made this book possible, and they didn't even get to see the fruition of their prayers. Will we be that type of woman for others that are coming behind us? I want to honor the women over fifty for saying yes all these years. Thank you for saying yes to doing hard things; thank you for saying yes to following God and creating roads and bridges we can now walk on.

What has God called you to say yes to? He has something that He is calling you to do. He has a mission and a plan for your life, and it's bigger than your right now. The future is in God's hands, but we can partner with Him by saying yes.

Yes to being present with our kids even after a sleepless night.

Yes to getting marriage counseling.

Yes to getting help for our body-image issues.

Yes to forgiving a girlfriend even though she stabbed us in the back.

Yes to supporting other women in our world.

Yes to encouraging the next generation.

You may feel like you're being attacked with the spirit of death. You may feel like a death threat hangs over your life and your mind. But the Bible encourages us to remember our eternal life with Christ: "I will not die, but live, and tell of the works of the LORD" (Psalm 118:17, NASB). For you, saying yes might mean staying in the fight and remembering that God has already said yes to you and that your future is in His powerful, loving hands.

Every negative word that has ever been spoken over you is broken in the name of Jesus. You can step into your future with confidence.

You may need to say yes to endurance, to not quitting. Or yes to getting the help you need to finish what you began. Or yes to getting started—starting that non-profit, that song, that business idea.

The world needs what God has placed inside you. And saying yes to God will let it shine.

Let's Pray

Father God, I thank You that You have said yes to me, to my life, to my salvation, to being my present help no matter what challenges I'm facing. I thank You for the conviction that today I can say yes to You. I thank You that the Spirit of the living God is in me and that You're going to use me and the sisterhood of Your daughters to change this world for Your glory. Help me step into this season with boldness. Help me step into this season with faith. Guide me in doing what You've called me to do. Whatever it is You ask of me, help me say yes.

15

NIGHT VISION

Recently, Earl and I were returning from a quick trip, and we saw Stevie Wonder at the airport. Earl's a practical joker, so when he pointed Stevie Wonder out to me, I said, "Yeah, right. Whatever. That man is not Stevie Wonder; he's just a guy with braids." Earl kept insisting that the man was Stevie Wonder, but again, he teases all the time. I've been married to him for all these years, and I still can't tell when he's being serious. So I decided to be bold and take a picture of the man. And sure enough, it really was him. When I texted my mom-in-law, who loves Stevie Wonder, she said, "That is not Stevie Wonder. He would not just be at the airport by himself." But he had a bodyguard and an assistant with him. I then started thinking about what it would be like to be blind. Stevie Wonder and others who are blind often rely on a guide to help them navigate a sight-dominant world.

If you've found yourself out walking late at night, you've experienced how your other senses—hearing, smell, and touch—become keener when you can't see as well. When we go through dark seasons in our lives, we might discover we hear God's voice in a different way.

Maybe right now you feel lost because you don't know what's next for your life, and that is driving you crazy. I get that! Or maybe you feel alone in just kind of a blah season. I get that too. God wants to speak to you during this time. He wants to give you clarity, and He wants to give you vision for your future to carry you through to the other side of this season.

Sometimes when our lives are dark, we run for cover until the storm is over. We just hide out. But what if we ran into the hard times and toward Jesus? What if we ran, saying, "God, I can't see. I don't know where I'm going, but I hear Your still, small voice. I know that You're going to lead me and guide me. During this time when I don't know if I should step forward, step right, or step left, I'm believing that I'm going to be able to hear from You like never before." This perspective will give us a different way of approaching times of darkness. These times could actually be when God wants to birth something in us.

We know that "the LORD gives sight to the blind" (Psalm 146:8, NIV). What if that means that He gives us insight and vision when we feel blind? God can give you vision for your future in times when you can't see in the darkness. Instead of approaching these times with despair, wait them out, saying, "God, what are You saying in this moment? How are You leading me? What are You bringing to life in me? What are You trying to show me? I can't see anything, so I'm just going to wait to hear what You have to say." We can draw great grace and strength from this humble and curious posture.

When I was going through a really tough time with some family drama, I told God, "I need a word. I need You to just drop something in my heart and in my spirit to carry me through this time. I need a word to stand on during this dark, troubling situation." He led me right to Isaiah 45:3: "I will give you treasures hidden in the darkness—secret riches. I will do this so you may know that I am the LORD, the God of Israel, the one who calls you by name." God is saying here, "I am going to give you treasures and beautiful things in times of darkness." Treasures are hidden below surface level, so you don't see them initially. You have to dig for treasure. God is saying, "When things get dark around you, when you feel like you can't see, and when you don't know which way to go, I'm going to give you treasures hidden in your season of darkness." Don't despise this dark time when you don't know what next step to take. Embrace it. You're not going to stay here forever. Just as the sun rises and sets every single day, this season will pass. We're guaranteed the grace to get through it.

We're always in a hurry to get out of the valley of shadows. We say, "Get me out of the valley, Lord, so I can get to the mountain. Get me out of the valley. Get me out of the valley." But God wants to do something in you while you're in the valley so that when you get to the mountain, you can stand strong and give Him the glory. While you're in the valley of the shadow of death and you can't see, He's birthing your calling. He's creating something for your future. He's giving you fresh vision and purpose. He will give you treasure. He knows your name, He knows your story, He knows your struggles, He knows what you're facing, and He cares. He loves you, He's going to see you through, and He wants to speak to you when you feel confused and discouraged or when you don't know where you're headed.

So many times throughout Scripture, God spoke at night. First Samuel records one particular time. Hannah was crying out to God for a baby. She had dealt with infertility for years, and she was bullied because of it. She made a promise to God that if He gave her a baby, she would dedicate him to God. God answered her prayer, and after her son was born, she took great care of Samuel and loved him. Hannah kept her vow and took Samuel to the tabernacle to be dedicated to the Lord and to grow up there and assist the priest Eli.[1]

First Samuel 3:1 says, "In those days messages from the LORD were very rare, and visions were quite uncommon." As I read that, I wondered why visions were rare during that time. Then I discovered that Eli's sons, who were also priests, were sinful and acting inappropriately.[2] God was silent, or perhaps He wasn't being heard.

Then one night the Lord called Samuel by name while he was sleeping. Samuel ran to Eli and asked, "Eli, did you call me?" Eli said, "Nope, go back to sleep." But Samuel kept hearing his name being called and kept asking Eli if he was calling for him. Finally, Eli realized who was trying to get Samuel's attention and instructed him to listen to God. The Lord called again, "Samuel! Samuel!" Then Samuel said, "Speak, your servant is listening" (verse 10). God called Samuel to become an amazing judge and prophet, and the messages of God were heard in the land once again because Samuel answered the call.

In your seasons of night, God is going to call you to something. He's going to stir something in you because you're going to hear His voice in new ways. Sometimes we think we get called when our lives are great or when all our i's are dotted and t's are crossed or when our lives are organized all neat and tidy. But God calls us in the night.

> *God called Samuel in the night, and He can call you during your night seasons too.*

It's so freeing and refreshing to know that we don't have to stay in the dark times forever. When your sisters are walking through dark times, stir up the faith and hope within them by saying, "God wants to give you vision and clarity in the night. He wants to solidify His call on your life. He wants to give you marching orders for your next season. Don't be so quick to get out of the valley and make it to the mountain, because He's going to give you instructions in the valley on how to handle the mountain." We need the vision that God is going to give us during the night seasons of our lives.

The more I looked, the more I saw God speaking words of hope and light in the night—even in the Christmas story: "That night there were shepherds staying in the fields nearby, guarding their flocks of sheep. Suddenly, an angel of the Lord appeared among them, and the radiance of the Lord's glory surrounded them" (Luke 2:8–9).

These shepherds were thinking it was going to be just an ordinary night of faithfully taking care of sheep. Your ordinary night could include putting your kids to bed. You could be graduating and entering into a new season of the ordinary. You could be loving and serving your husband in a marriage that seems ordinary. But suddenly, God shows up. The shepherds were faithful; they showed up. Sometimes we just have to show up. We have to show up in our friendships; we have to show up in our marriages; we have to show up to our jobs—because God is birthing something through our faithfulness. Your "suddenly" is coming in your consistency. Your "suddenly" is set in motion by your obedience. You don't know when your "suddenly" is going to hit. The shepherds didn't know. They just showed up to a regular night of tending sheep; then angels came from heaven, declaring that a child had been born and telling them to go see the child.

The shepherds were in the right place at the right time; they were obedient, faithful, and consistent. They weren't at church when their "suddenly" moment came; they were at work. For you, maybe that's being at your husband's side. For you, maybe that's being faithful in school. For you, it could be staying friends with a woman who needs you. For you, it could be exercising but still not losing weight. But before you know it, that moment is going to come and breakthrough is going to happen. Do you know what happened to those shepherds? They saw Jesus, then ran to tell everybody that their Savior had been born. When that moment comes, God is going to allow you to use your story to tell others about His faithfulness and His goodness, not so you can take credit but so you can give Him all the glory.

When you feel like you can't see, say, like Samuel, "Speak, your servant is listening." When you don't know what step to take, just show up. Show up to your job. Be present in your friendships. Be present in your marriage. Be present with God. Because this is the recipe for your moment to unfold. I just keep sensing that maybe you feel lost or don't know what's next and that's driving you crazy. But God knows your future. He has it ordered and mapped out. He knows when you're coming and where you're going. He's the Alpha and Omega, the beginning and end. He's not with us just on the mountain—He's there in the valley too.

I gathered some promises that I believe will give you the grace to walk through a hard time of not knowing what's next. I'm believing that, through these scriptures, God is going to give you vision when you're walking through the night.

Psalm 119:105 says, "Your word is a lamp for my feet, a light on my path" (NIV). God's Word is our guide to help us see in times of darkness. So keep His Word close to you because He'll be able to help you navigate the dark times.

> *Don't come out of a dark time with nothing; come out with spiritual treasure.*

In Psalm 32:8, the Lord said, "I will guide you along the best pathway for your life. I will advise you and watch over you." I love that.

First Corinthians 2:9 says, "No eye has seen, no ear has heard, and no mind has imagined what God has prepared for those who love him." He loves you. He has an amazing future ready for you. Don't despise the valley seasons. Don't despise the times when you can't see. Embrace them because they last only for a season.

Why not get through the season with more faith? Why not get through it with more wisdom? Why not get through it with more vision for your future? Don't settle for nothing, as though you got robbed of that season of your life. Come out on the other side with new strength, new insights, and refined trust in God.

My son and I both faced intense physical sickness when we moved to Dallas in 2011. There were ER visits, two surgeries, and bed rest. I wouldn't want to repeat that season, nor would I wish it on anyone. But I will say, because of that very dark time, I gained some spiritual stamina. I learned to cry out to God, because my life depended on it. I learned to have compassion and empathy for others facing hard seasons. I learned not to repeat cute Christian bumper sticker phrases but to be present for people even without using words. And I learned to rely on God for the breath in my lungs and for the endurance to stand when so much around me seemed to be crumbling. I found encouragement in Luke 21:28: "When all these things begin to happen, stand and look up, for your salvation is near!"

You want to be stronger, wiser, more focused, and more in love with Jesus. You want to be more confident that without Him you can do nothing and more certain of His promises and His Word.

And in the meantime, while you're waiting for the night to end and a sunnier season to dawn in your life, keep your ears open to hear God's voice in the dark. You can trust that He's with you, that He's doing more than you see.

Let's Pray

Jesus, I'm feeling blind, but I know You're birthing something. I'm feeling weak, but I know a breakthrough is coming. I don't know which way to go, but I know You are the way. Please help me not to give up but to press into Your presence like never before. Help me become the woman of God that You've called me to be. Give me eyes to see the future that You have for me. As I go about my day, open my eyes to see the lost, the hurting, and the broken. Wherever I go, please urge me to declare the goodness of my Savior and not myself. May my life be a city on a hill; may I live for Your fame and not my own. And may this change in me ignite change in my generation.

16

POWER IN THE SEED

Our eight-year-old, Grayson, brought me some seeds and told me that he was going to plant an apple tree. I thought that was so cute. He planted it and we watered it. Every day, he would get frustrated because a tree hadn't grown yet. We ended up selling that house and moving, so we never got to see what became of those apple seeds, but I like to imagine the next family discovering a little sapling in their new yard.

We get frustrated with our lives, but God knows the potential of seeds. He's tending to the seeds in your life in ways that you don't even know. Sometimes we look at the seeds of our current season and feel as if they aren't enough. We look at the seeds of our relationships, compare them with others, and think our relationships aren't enough. We look at the seeds of our kids, compare them with other families, and think our children aren't enough. I want to tell you that the future is in the seed. Don't despise small beginnings, and don't despise your seed season, because the reason we're here today is that so many women planted seeds of prayer, peace, and hope before us and we're reaping the harvest. Now it's our turn to steward the seeds that God has given us, because His plan for the world isn't done.

> *Don't despise your seed season.*
> *He's just getting started.*

I'm going to challenge us and encourage us to steward the seeds in our possession, because we've been called for such a time as this. I know sometimes we all think, *What can God do with this life? My friends on social media seem like they have it all together. Their pictures are always perfect. Everybody's hair is just right. The filter's just right.* Then we look at ourselves with sleep in our eyes and coffee spills on our pajamas, and we think, *My life's not worth anything.* But I'm here to tell you that it is. We can't compare ourselves with pictures on social media, because they're not real. Our standard is the Word of God, which is the mirror that we're called to look into. If you're dealing with any type of mess in your health, your family, your finances, or your business, God can breathe life into it, and that situation will yield a supernatural harvest. Don't despise your seed season; see it as a key to your future and as a gift for the next generation. The girls coming up after us are watching how we conduct our friendships, they're watching our text responses, and they're watching our selfies. Then they're emulating us. We want the seven-, eight-, nine-, ten-, fifteen-, and twenty-year-olds to know their value in

Christ. We want them to know that they don't have to starve themselves or compare themselves with anyone, because they're fear-
fully and wonderfully made.[1] They're watching us because it's our
turn. Are you ready to steward the seeds that God has given you?

God talked about a seed in the very beginning in the Garden of
Eden. Genesis 3:15 reads, "I will put enmity between you and the
woman, and between your seed and her Seed; He shall bruise your
head, and you shall bruise His heel" (NKJV). Adam and Eve had
everything they could have ever wanted. God gave them everything
in the garden, except for just one tree. They lived in a beautiful
place but still had their eyes on what they couldn't have. How many
of us have been planted in a great family but have our eyes on the
apple we can't have? How many of us have great relationships but
have our eyes on the relationships we don't have? Adam and Eve
focused on what they couldn't have. Then the Enemy came and
tempted them with the very thing they were forbidden to have.
There's nothing better than what you have right now. The life that
God has given you is a gift, and if you plant in it, water it, and
steward it well, you will reap a harvest.

Sin entered the world in the garden, but God always had a plan.
Even when Adam and Eve turned their backs on Him, He still had
a plan. His plan was Jesus Christ, who was placed as a seed in a
woman. Jesus defeated death, hell, and the grave. He is our plan
for freedom and salvation. God trusted a woman with the seed of
Jesus Christ just like He's trusted you with various seeds. Guess
what your seeds are going to do? They're going to bruise the head
of the Enemy. The seed of your college season can bruise the head
of the Enemy. The seed of your marriage can bruise the head of
the Enemy. The seed of your stay-at-home-mom life—where you

feel like, *I'm so bored. I miss working. I'm so sick of these kids*—can bruise the head of the Enemy.

I just want to encourage you that God sees you even if your situation seems minuscule to you. His eyes are on you every single day, and He's proud of you. He's pleased with you. He loves you.

Maybe you wonder, *Why would He choose a seed?* Well, seeds are packed with potential, and that same potential exists inside the seeds that God has given you. Potential lies in every season.

I think sometimes we want what other people have attained and are discontent with our own lives in comparison. What we don't know is that person stayed at their God-assigned post for thirty years. What we don't see are those nights that they didn't sleep and laid hands on that husband who seemed like he'd never go to church. What we don't see is how they paced the hall outside their children's rooms, praying, "I plead the blood of Jesus Christ over my children and pray that no weapon formed against them shall prosper. I declare that they are the head and not the tail." We see these parents' mature, respectful children, but we don't see the seed season. I want to encourage you to enjoy the seed season. Don't get annoyed with it, and don't regret it, because this season is an opportunity for God to work.

Keep your childlike faith in Him, and don't give up. He wants to breathe life on every single seed that you steward. See your frustrations as seeds. Speak life to them, treasure them, guard them, pray over them, and don't give up hope.

One of my girlfriends, Betsy Baldwin, is a wedding coordinator. She creates detailed floral designs for all the beautiful weddings that she plans. Many of you already have Pinterest pages for your wedding and have already chosen your flower arrangements, your colors, and your dress, but you don't even have a man yet. That's okay; you can dream. But so many times we focus on the desired outcome. We see those beautiful centerpieces. We see the bouquets. We see the flowers and want that beautiful ceremony. But guess what? Betsy sat at a table for hours picking every single dead leaf and every single thorn from the flowers. The flowers didn't start in beautiful arrangements. The marriage that I have now didn't begin this way. It was a seed. I just want you to know that if you steward your seed well, something beautiful will unfold. We have to plant our seeds and steward them well. We can't give up or leave our post. The Enemy lures us into quitting because we see our relationships, jobs, or dreams only in seed form, but bouquets come from beautiful flower fields that began as seeds.

> *Don't compare your current seeds to another's bouquet.*

I don't know what is in seed form in your life right now. I don't know what land in your heart feels like a desert wasteland, but I just want you to know that God is calling us to steward our seed seasons well because a harvest is waiting. We can't despise the little. We can't minimize the little, because the future is in the seed. God wants to give us hope, peace, and joy. But those fruits of the Spirit come not by idolizing the bouquet but by getting our hands dirty in the planting. Those virtues come when we don't give up. They come in prayer. They come when we see the potential in something as small as a seed.

Maybe you need to be reminded that your life's not over. Your seeds mean something. Think about your marriage, family, and friends. Think about your college education. Think about your thought life. Think about what's burdening you. Those are all seeds. See them in the same way that God sees them. Pray over those seeds and trust Him. Maybe you've left an angry husband, and you were afraid to return home. God sees that seed. Maybe you have some ill-mannered, disrespectful children, and you wonder if there's hope that they will change. God sees that seed. Maybe you're stewarding a beautiful business, but no growth is occurring. God sees that seed. Maybe you're attempting to think life-giving thoughts by soaking in the truths of this book, but the old thoughts are trying to push the new mindset out. God sees that seed. He sees what's plaguing your mind, and He says, "Sweetheart, I'm renewing your mind. Sweetheart, your thoughts are not My thoughts. Sweetheart, your ways are not My ways. Sweetheart, I think higher. I think better. I think greater for you. Don't settle. Steward that seed."

Don't settle.
Steward that seed.

"The LORD will guide you continually," reads Isaiah 58:11, "giving you water when you are dry and restoring your strength. You will be like a well-watered garden, like an ever-flowing spring." Do you feel dry? God wants to restore your strength.

God sees your tears. He sees your doubts. He sees your fears. What seems insignificant now, when carefully prayed over, planted, and cultivated, can become a stunning garden.

Remain on the Vine

In order for us to bloom and bear fruit, we have to abide in the Vine, who is Jesus. Reading God's Word is the catalyst we need to abide in Him.

Galatians 5:22–23 says, "The Holy Spirit produces this kind of fruit in our lives: love, joy, peace, patience, kindness, goodness, faithfulness, gentleness, and self-control." It might seem like a lot of growth to do, but this fruit grows all together like a grape cluster. Ask God to give you fresh revelation on one, then another one, and then the next one.

God wants to help you bear fruit in all your seasons. In your dark times of discouragement—when you're frustrated and overwhelmed, when you don't have enough money or think your life's not where it should be—you might wonder how you can bear fruit. But you can always bear fruit if you abide in Him and His Word abides in you.

Bearing fruit happens not by accident but by intention.

My husband is my very best friend. I love him more than anything besides Jesus. When we started dating, we decided to apply John 15 to our lives. We knew we wanted our relationship to bear good fruit, because few relationships around us, dating or married, were healthy. We decided that we wanted our relationship to inspire hope, so we studied John 15 while we were dating, but we've found that the principles for bearing fruit apply to all areas of our lives.

John 15 says that in order to bear fruit, we have to remain on the Vine. The more we stay connected to God's presence, the more able we are to bear good and lasting fruit. A vine gives strength and nutrients to the branches. God wants to reinforce our branches so they can hold the fruit that He's given us without breaking.

There in John 15, Jesus is saying to us, "Remain in me, and I will remain in you" (verse 4). We hold on to God for dear life because when we remain in Him, we live fruitful lives. That's how we endure storms. That's how we endure the shade. We hold on to God for dear life. I think we hold on to people or our phones too much. Phones are addictive. You set your phone down; you can't find it; then you start getting jittery. You can't concentrate in a conversation because you're in a panic over your lost phone. But sometimes we have to put the phone down. We have to remain in Him because that's how we're going to bear fruit.

Jesus continued, "A branch cannot produce fruit if it is severed from the vine. . . . Yes, I am the vine; you are the branches. Those who remain in me, and I in them, will produce much fruit. For apart from me you can do nothing" (verses 4–5). We're more fruitful when we do life together and put our hope in God. We have to trust Him and ask Him to water us through His Word so that we can bear fruit.

Let Yourself Be Pruned

We have to be willing to let God cut away dead branches. He prunes us out of love, removing the branches that don't bear fruit so that the ones that do will produce even more. Don't despise the cutting seasons of your life. Don't despise the times when you feel like you have few friends, because God is cutting your life back so that you can bear more fruit. Don't despise the pruning in your life, because it's going to take you to a richer, deeper place. Through His pruning, God gets the focus off the thing that we thought we couldn't live without. We have to put our focus back on Him because our lives should declare His glory. So sometimes He just has to shake up our lives to remind us that He's God, that He's in control, and that our focus needs to be on Him.

Give Your Fruit Away

Sometimes we hold on to the gifts in our lives because we want them for ourselves, but other people need the blessing of your gift. People can be blessed by your organizational skills, your musical gift, your smile, or your ability to stand and be faithful. Thank God for people who just show up and stand with you. They don't even need to say the right words because their showing up is a gift. Just being present in somebody's life is a gift.

When someone's going through a tough time like depression or divorce, they just need someone by their side. I promise you— there isn't one thing you're facing or one battle you're fighting that someone else hasn't gone through. But the Enemy tries to isolate us by making us think that we're alone in our struggle when so many people struggle with the same issue. We need to remember that we're in this battle together.

As you trust God with your battle and are vulnerable with others, ask someone who's already been victorious in a similar battle to pray for you and encourage you. They will be able to say, "I might be bearing fruit right now, but you didn't see me when I was in the shade and couldn't see that this harvest time was coming. You didn't see me when I thought about giving up. I don't know how, but fruit still grew in the shade." Some of the darkest times of my life, when I felt like God had forgotten about me, were the most fruitful, so don't despise the tough times.

When we remain in God, there's no dream so big that He can't fulfill it. When we abide in Him, there's no desire or passion we have that will scare Him. However, that dream, desire, or passion will break us if we put our hope in its fulfillment and not in Him.

How do we remain on the Vine and bear good fruit? The concept of reading God's Word seems so basic, but there is power in Scripture. Chains fall, blind eyes see, and deaf ears hear through the power of the Word of God. When we remain in Him by reading His Word and applying it to our lives and our situations, we make a difference in the world.

I still believe in the gifts of the Spirit. I still believe in the fruit of the Spirit. I still believe that God can resurrect dead situations. I still believe that He can take a girl who's hopeless, broken, and downcast and give her the joy of the Lord. I still believe that God can speak peace to someone who's so anxiety-ridden that they can't even leave their home. I still believe that Jesus can heal anyone who feels so heavy or plagued by darkness that they can't think about others or see a way out. I still believe that the Word of God and God's presence can change your situation so you can bear fruit. You might feel like a tree that is dry and fruitless with scrawny branches and withering leaves, but right now, God's Word is falling on the tree of your life. He's reminding you that you will remain and that He will allow the rivers of His presence to flow into your life so you will bear fruit. Jeremiah 17:7 says, "Blessed is the one who trusts in the LORD" (NIV). Are you trusting in God?

He's called us to be "like trees replanted in Eden, putting down roots near the rivers" (verse 8, MSG). This verse is a picture of us flourishing without worry even through the hottest of summers. You may be feeling the heat or pressure of life, but God wants to give you grace. You're not going to lose your mind. You're not going to lose your salvation. You're not going to lose your peace. You're going to trust and abide in Him, and you're going to bear much fruit.

Let's Pray

Thank You, Jesus, that as Your daughter my life is not defined by my past but is filled with faith for the present. Lead and guide me, keep me close, equip me for the road ahead, and give me a prophetic word for what's around the corner. Bless and strengthen my family and friendships. I pray for the sisterhood of the daughters of God. Propel us into our futures with confidence and grace. May we stay filled with wonder and awe and have a divine expectation for what's ahead in every area of our lives. As curveballs come our way, may each of us com-

mit to declare emphatically that You are with us, You will

never fail us, and You, the Most High God, have pre-

pared us for what's to come. Go before Your girls, Jesus,

and may we live with our eyes forever fixed on You.

Amen.

17

PLANTED TO FLOURISH

May is the happiest time of the year for me because my birthday, my wedding anniversary, and Mother's Day are all included. Every May, I have this extra special time with God when I pray, read my Bible, and say, "God, speak to me about this upcoming year. What do You think it's going to look like? Where do You want my focus? What words do You want me to meditate on throughout the year?" This year, the word that lifted off the page to me was *flourish*. I felt like God was inspiring me to encourage every woman around me to flourish in all that God has called her to be.

This is our season to flourish. To flourish means to break forth or to bloom.[1] God is going to call us to do this. Flowers in full bloom are gorgeous. You just can't help but notice them. When you see flowers or gardens, remember that God is whispering to you, "I've started something in you, and, girl, this is your season to flourish." Some of us might be thinking, *Yes, I'm ready, willing, and able. This is going to be my season to flourish.* Then others of us are think-ing, *You don't even know what it took to get me to pick up this book. I'm barely holding on by a thread.* I want you to know that this word is for all of us and that God is going to do something in all our hearts. Just open up. Breathe in and breathe out, exhale and relax, and you will be surprised at what begins to bloom.

Psalm 92:12–13 says, "The godly"—and he's talking about all of us who love God—"will flourish like palm trees and grow strong like the cedars of Lebanon. For they are transplanted to the LORD's own house. They flourish in the courts of our God." When I read that, I thought, *What does it mean to flourish like a palm tree?*

Strong Enough to Bend

Palm trees bend, but they don't break. Situations in life may require us to bend, but we don't have to break. In the 1970s, Hur-ricane Frederic hit the Gulf Coast, and the indigenous pine trees there just snapped under the pressure. But the palm trees bent. That could be our lives. When the storms hit and the wind and waves come, say, "I'm planted on Christ's solid rock. I'm going to stay planted in the Word. I'm going to stay planted in a church." You may bend so low that you almost taste dirt, but you don't have to break. We flourish by staying planted.

For some of us, it's so easy to be shallow and not grow roots because we've been hurt before. We make excuses for not digging deep because we're afraid we'll be hurt again. But we have to go deep in our relationship with God and others because those rela-tional roots will enable us to stand when the winds howl or the storms of life crash against us unexpectedly. If our roots grow deep, we have something to hold on to.

There is no formula for a mess-proof life, but when we are rooted in God and the wind comes and the waves rise, we won't break.

> *If our roots are deep, we can withstand whatever comes our way.*

Maybe you've been through hell. Maybe an important relationship didn't work out the way you planned or words spoken over you caused emotional or spiritual death in you. But because you're rooted, you're still standing. You declared, "I may be a little bent, but I'm not broken. I'm not going to let this snap me." Sometimes we get surprised when we have to bend, when situations don't turn out the way we planned, but if our roots are deep, we're going to be able to withstand whatever comes our way.

Flourish in Replanting

Psalm 92:13 says, "They are transplanted to the LORD's own house." God replants us because some of us have roots in the soil of wrong relationships. We shouldn't be in that relationship pot or this particular soil. Some of us have put our roots down in unhealthy mindsets or thought processes for too long. That soil isn't the right soil for our minds.

God supernaturally takes us from an unhealthy place of planting and plants us in a healthier place so that we can flourish. When a plant is stuffed in a pot that's not big enough to hold it, its roots hang out everywhere. Some of you feel claustrophobic in your life; you feel trapped and you can't get out. I believe that God is breaking your pot and is going to plant you in fresh soil.

God's breaking is exciting, but it's also going to be messy. It's not easy and glamorous to go from one pot of soil to another. Dirt gets everywhere. The process is messy, but it's worth it because our growth can be stunted when we stay in the wrong pot or the wrong soil. You can grow only so far when you're planted in a pot that's stifling you. I dare you to get into a bigger pot, then see how you're able to spread out and how people notice something different about you. You won't seem the same, because you're growing in grace and flourishing with confidence.

Crack your pot; then get rid of it.

Flourish in the Desert

Deserts are dry and desperate for water, but palm trees can thrive in deserts, and we can as well. Sometimes we go through desert or wilderness situations, and we think our lives are over. We might think, *I'm in the desert. How am I going to grow? How is God going to speak to me or use me?* I promise you—you can flourish in the desert seasons of your life.

In the winter, my hands get really dry and crack. I have to use a lot of lotion. I mean a lot. A few years ago, I went to Walgreens one morning and didn't have time to put on lotion. As I was checking out, the cashier said, "Wow, you look a lot older than your driver's license says because your hands are so wrinkly."

Yep, that really happened. People will just say crazy stuff.

Well, sometimes we think that God can use us only when we're at our best or feeling strong and encouraged, but we can flourish even in hard times.

Jesus is familiar with the wilderness. There was such an amazing, powerful moment when He was baptized by His cousin John the Baptist. In the hearing of the crowd gathered at the river, God declared from heaven, "You are my dearly loved Son, and you bring me great joy" (Mark 1:11). But Scripture records that, right after that high moment, "the Spirit then compelled Jesus to go into the wilderness" (verse 12). Jesus has suffered through times when He felt forgotten, alone, and frustrated. Wild animals were prowling in the wilderness with Him. Jesus was isolated, but it was in that desert that He passed many character tests. It was in that desert that God sent angels to comfort Him.[2] So you may be in the wilderness, but God is sending angels to comfort you, to care for you, and to strengthen you.

Hosea 13:5 says, "I took care of you in the wilderness, in that dry and thirsty land." God is going to take care of you in your wilderness season. It may feel dry. You may be tired and thirsty, but God knows you. He sees you. He hasn't forgotten you. He knows every hair on your head. He sees your pain and frustration. Maybe you're in a high season of life but have a family member that's in the wilderness. God sees their pain. He sees their frustration. The Lord spoke to Moses in the desert.[3] He can speak to you in your desert, and He can speak through you in the deserts of your friends and family. He can drop words into your heart or send people across your path that act as water to your soul. That phone call, that text message, that sermon, or that smile can be your water in the desert. God is familiar with and unafraid of the deserts of our lives.

Even in your desert season,

I dare you to flourish.

I'm committed to continue flourishing. I'm choosing to stay planted by water. What does that look like for me? For one example, I've been married for twenty-five years, and I've made it a point to keep asking women who have gone before me for wisdom and to listen for insights into any blind spots I might have. I went through a season when I felt like I had arrived, but the truth is, I will never arrive. I will always be on this journey. I fight to stay by streams of water so that my leaves won't wither in marriage or any other area.[4] That is my prayer for you as well. Fight to keep growing, learning, and becoming more like Jesus.

Some things you can learn only when you're in the desert. You're going to learn crazy, amazing stuff about yourself and Jesus that He can share with you only in dry, slow seasons. Don't be afraid of the wilderness. God will take care of you. He will pour into you. He will strengthen you. You will come back stronger than you could ever imagine. And while you wait to get through, you can pray, "God, I'm not alone. I've got You. I have a whole sisterhood cheering me on and praying for me."

Only God can cause you to flourish. The fact that so many of you have survived all the trials and heartaches you've been through is a miracle. Don't forget that. I think we can get so used to surviving that we forget to look around and notice how we're already thriving. Share the miracle of God's work in your life as a way of reminding yourself and others that flourishing is possible in every season. Flourishing doesn't mean being fake or saying that something is good when it's not. It's being real, not isolating yourself. It's being planted around other people so that you can flourish together.

Painting a picture of what this looks like, the prophet Isaiah said,

> Energize the limp hands,
>> strengthen the rubbery knees.
> Tell fearful souls,
>> "Courage! Take heart!
> GOD is here, right here,
>> on his way to put things right
> And redress all wrongs.
>> He's on his way! He'll save you!"
>
> Blind eyes will be opened.
>> deaf ears unstopped,
> Lame men and women will leap like deer,
>> the voiceless break into song.
> Springs of water will burst out in the wilderness,
>> streams flow in the desert.
> Hot sands will become a cool oasis,
>> thirsty ground a splashing fountain.
> Even lowly jackals will have water to drink,
>> and barren grasslands flourish richly.
>> (Isaiah 35:3–7, MSG)

God is energizing anyone who doesn't feel like they can lift their hands. He's strengthening the weak knees. For any of you dealing with fear, God speaks to you, "Have courage, beautiful."

God is with you. He's right beside you. He's on the move.

Many of you have obeyed God simply by reading this book. While you're sitting here reading, He's putting things right on your behalf because He's that amazing. You feel like you've been blind in a certain situation, but Isaiah reminds us that God opens our eyes.

Some of you need to start singing again because you stopped singing and dreaming years ago. However, God is declaring that you're getting your voice back.

What's dead in you? What's barren in you? God is saying, "Stay flexible. Keep bending; don't break. I'm pouring into you. I'm growing and strengthening you. Soon your palm tree will stand so strong that others will find shade beneath it."

We are brilliant; we are fearless; we are strong; we are sought after; we are altogether lovely; our past and the words of others don't define us. No matter what our birth certificates say, we have royal blood in our veins. Our identity is in Jesus. And as His daughters, we will walk this earth with purpose because we were made for this!

Let's Pray

Thank You, Jesus, for every one of Your daughters that

You have made for this very moment. I thank You that, in

this moment, You are bringing life to those things that

seem dead or barren within me and within each of us. We are blossoming. You are strengthening us to stand tall. I thank You that this is our moment to flourish. Lead us and go before us, and help us flourish in the good and bad times. I thank You that we are not alone but that You are with us and that You love us. In Jesus's name, amen.

AFTERWORD

As we part ways here, I pray for you, friend. I speak calmness over you. I speak peace over you. I speak strength over you. I speak hope over you. I pray that you bear fresh fruit in each season.

You were born royal; you were made for such a time as this. May your life be filled with the goodness of God. May your footsteps be ordered by the Lord. May healing, purpose, and confidence permeate every area of your life.

I want to prophesy over you as you finish these pages. You are stepping into a new season of greatness, strength, boldness, faith, joy, and supernatural peace. He has gone before you. In the name of Jesus, no weapon formed against you or your family shall prosper. God has handpicked you to help usher in a value revolution in your life and in the life of every woman in your sphere. I'm believing that every word on the pages of this book, fused with the workings of the precious Holy Spirit, were able to wash over and renew your mind. I'm believing that you are positioned to take new steps of freedom as you walk out this beautiful, epic call.

With so much love,

Oneka

ACKNOWLEDGMENTS

To my amazing husband, Earl. Thank you for loving me, believing in me, and always speaking life over me. You are my very best friend, and I am honored to be your wife. This book wouldn't have been possible without your constant love and support. You always pull out the best in me. I can't believe I get to be on this journey of a lifetime with you. I love, respect, cherish, and admire you.

To my smart, handsome boys, Parker and Grayson. Thank you for releasing me and being patient with me as I wrote this book. I love being your mom. My prayer for you is that you will always honor and value every girl in your life. Through the lens of this book, may God give you a picture of the beautiful gift that every woman on the planet is.

To my daughter, Elle. My star. My heart. My mini me. I love you with all my heart, and I pray that you always walk in the confidence that your dad and I have placed in you. May you always know your value and worth, and may you always see yourself the way God sees you.

I am so thankful for my beautiful mother, Rosa. Thank you for showing me what it means to be strong, loving, compassionate, and others oriented. Your constant example of grace and sacrifice taught me, at a young age, that anything is possible when we believe.

To my mom-in-law, Diane. You exemplify strength and courage. Your presence makes everything sweeter. Thank you for surrounding me in every season. Thank you for your constant encouragement, love, and support. You are the best Nana our kids could ask for.

To my beautiful church family, Shoreline City. It is my complete joy and honor to be your pastor. Thank you for cheering me on during this incredible church journey. You are forever written on the tablet of my heart. You are part of this book's journey wherever it goes, because I've shared these exact words with you over the years. I love you, and I will never stop fighting for you and believing in you. Together, let's keep bringing heaven to earth.

NOTES

1: YOUR TIME IS NOW

1. "What Is the Creed?," Shoreline City Church, www
   .shorelinecity.church/whoweare.

2: HONORED BY GOD

1. Matthew 5:14.
2. Barbara Leonhard, "Jesus' Extraordinary Treatment of
   Women," Franciscan Media, November 2017, www
   .franciscanmedia.org/st-anthony-messenger/jesus
   -extraordinary-treatment-of-women.
3. John 8:3–11.
4. Luke 8:43–48.
5. Luke 8:41–42, 49–56.
6. Luke 13:10–16.

7.   Matthew 28:8–9.

8.   Matthew 28:10.

9.   John 4:28–30.

10. John 8:3–11.

11. Deuteronomy 28:13, NKJV.

12. Philippians 4:13, NKJV.

13. Edward Mote, "My Hope Is Built on Nothing Less," 1834, https://hymnary.org/text/my_hope_is_built_on_nothing_less.

14. Cody Carnes, "Firm Foundation (He Won't)," by Cody Carnes, Austin Davis, and Chandler Moore, track 4 on *Firm Foundation (Live)*, Sparrow Records, 2023.

15. Proverbs 18:24, NIV.

3: A NEW NAME

1.   Genesis 17:5–6.

2.   "Genesis 17:5," Biblica, accessed October 23, 2023, www.biblica.com/bible/?osis=niv:Genesis%2017:5.

3.   "Sarai Meaning," Abarim Publications, accessed October 11, 2023, www.abarim-publications.com/Meaning/Sarai.html.

4.   "Sarah Meaning," Abarim Publications, accessed October 11, 2023, www.abarim-publications.com/Meaning/Sarah.html.

5.   John 15:16.

6.   Jeremiah 29:11.

7.   Barbara F. McManus, "Roman Nomenclature," VRoma, updated November 2007, http://vroma.org/vromans/bmcmanus/roman_names.html.

8.   "The Civil War and Emancipation," PBS, accessed October 11, 2023, www.pbs.org/wgbh/aia/part4/4p2967.html.

9.   2 Corinthians 3:17.

10. Ephesians 2:8.

11. 2 Corinthians 5:21, NIV.

12. Matthew 5:14.

13. Galatians 3:13, NIV.

14. Jeremiah 31:3.

15. 1 Peter 2:9.

16. 1 John 5:4, NIV.

17. Romans 8:16.

18. Galatians 5:1.

4: DAUGHTER OF THE KING

1. Esther 2–5.

2. Mark 6:22 (AMP) refers to her as Salome, but in the New Living Translation, she is called Herodia, her mother's name.

3. "Strong's G2266," Blue Letter Bible, accessed October 12, 2023, www.blueletterbible.org/lexicon/g2266/kjv/tr/0-1.

4. Mike Campbell, "Salome," Behind the Name, last modified November 20, 2020, www.behindthename.com/name /salome.

5. 1 Peter 2:9, NKJV.

6. Isaiah 41:9, NIV.

7. 1 Corinthians 6:20, ESV.

5: BIRTHRIGHT OF PEACE

1. Philippians 4:7, ESV.

2. James Strong, *The New Strong's Expanded Exhaustive Concordance of the Bible*, s.v. "eirēnē" (Nashville, Tenn.: Thomas Nelson, 2010).

3. 2 Corinthians 12:9, NIV.

4. Philippians 4:7.

5. 2 Corinthians 5:17, NKJV.

6: MADE FOR VICTORY

1. Judges 4:4.

2. Mike Campbell, "Deborah," Behind the Name, last modified May 29, 2020, www.behindthename.com/name/deborah.

3. Cornelius a Lapide, quoted in F. W. Farrar, "Judges 4:4," in *Ellicott's Commentary for English Readers,* ed. Charles John Ellicott, Bible Hub, accessed October 13, 2023, https://biblehub.com /judges/4-4.htm.

4. "The Importance of Pollinators," U.S. Department of Agriculture, accessed October 13, 2023, www.usda.gov/peoples -garden/pollinators.

5. Laura Bortolotti and Cecilia Costa, "Chemical Communication in the Honey Bee Society," in *Neurobiology of Chemical Communication,* ed. Carla Mucignat-Caretta (Boca Raton, Fla.: CRC, 2014), www.ncbi.nlm.nih.gov/books/NBK200983.

7: GIVE ME ALSO

1. John 8:36, NIV.

2. Deuteronomy 21:17.

3. Genesis 25:24–34.

4. Genesis 27:1–45.

5. Ephesians 1:14.

8: EQUIPPED TO FIGHT

1. Psalm 118:17.

2. James 4:14, NKJV.

3. *Rocky*, directed by John G. Avildsen (Chartoff-Winkler Productions, 1976).

4. "Ronda Rousey's Secret to the Perfect Arm Bar: Rowdy's Places," video, 1:51, October 7, 2021, www.youtube.com /watch?v=hujNNhshiYU.

5. Ramona Shelburne, interviewed by ESPN, "Shelburne Says Rousey Fight Was Over Before It Started," ESPN, www.espn .com/video/clip/_/id/18381422.

6. "Strong's H5849," Blue Letter Bible, accessed October 16, 2023, www.blueletterbible.org/lexicon/h5849/kjv/wlc/0-1.

9: GIFTED TO LEAD

1. John 13:4–5.

2. *Failure to Launch*, directed by Tom Dey (Hollywood, Calif.: Paramount Pictures, 2006).

3. John 3:30, NKJV.

10: CROWNED TO SERVE

1. Luke 8:2–3.

2. Acts 16:14; 17:4, 12; 18:24–26.

3. Catherine Kroeger, "The Neglected History of Women in the Early Church," *Christian History*, 1988, Christian History Institute, https://christianhistoryinstitute.org/magazine/article /women-in-the-early-church.

4. John 10:31–33.

5. John 12:1.

6. John 12:2–3.

7. "Jewish Practices and Rituals: Covering of the Head," Jewish Virtual Library, accessed October 17, 2023, www.jewishvirtual library.org/covering-of-the-head.

8. John 12:5.

9. John 13:12–14.

10. John 13:15.

11: CALLED TO GATHER

1. Deuteronomy 31:8, NIV.

2. Ephesians 3:20, NKJV.

3. Luke 8:2–3.

4. Hebrews 12:1, NIV.

12: BE STILL IN THE MIDDLE

1. Dictionary.com, s.v. "still," accessed October 18, 2023, www
   .dictionary.com/browse/still.

2. Dictionary.com, s.v. "still."

3. Ephesians 3:20, NKJV.

13: WORSHIP IN THE BATTLE

1. "Strong's H3166," Blue Letter Bible, accessed October 19,
   2023, www.blueletterbible.org/lexicon/h3166/kjv/wlc/0-1.

2. Chris Tomlin, "How Great Is Our God," by Chris Tomlin,
   Jesse Reeves, and Ed Cash, track 3 on *Arriving*, Sparrow
   Records, 2004.

14: YOUR WORD IS YES

1. Colossians 1:27, NIV.

2. Deuteronomy 31:8, NIV.

3. Jeremiah 29:11.

4. Luke 12:7.

5. Exodus 2:1–10.

15: NIGHT VISION

1. 1 Samuel 1:1–28.

2. 1 Samuel 2:12–17.

16: POWER IN THE SEED

1. Psalm 139:14, NIV.

17: PLANTED TO FLOURISH

1. "Strong's H6524," Blue Letter Bible, accessed October 20, 2023, www.blueletterbible.org/lexicon/h6524/kjv/wlc/0-1.

2. Mark 1:13.

3. Numbers 3:14.

4. Psalm 1:3, NIV.

ABOUT THE AUTHOR

Oneka McClellan is a writer and speaker and, alongside her husband, she's pastor of Shoreline City Church's domestic and international campuses. Oneka and Earl have been married for more than twenty-five years and live in Dallas, Texas, with their three beautiful children—Parker, Grayson, and Elle. With a passion for sisterhood, Oneka has challenged the way women think about themselves by pioneering a value revolution that now spans the globe through a variety of creative and ministry initiatives. Oneka has a dynamic personality, creative vision, prophetic gift, and passion for God. She has propelled countless lives, marriages, teams, and churches into their God-given destinies.

ABOUT THE TYPE

This book was set in Mrs. Eaves, a typeface designed in 1996 by Zuzana Licko (b.1961) for Emigre graphics. Mrs. Eaves was styled after printed samples of Baskerville, accentuating the warmth and character that lead type imprints on paper. The typeface is named after Sarah Eaves, John Baskerville's wife and former housekeeper.